The Common Sense Guide to Leadership

The Common Sense Guide to Leadership

Yesterday's Values for Today's Leader

John F. Sullivan

iUniverse, Inc.
New York Lincoln Shanghai

The Common Sense Guide to Leadership
Yesterday's Values for Today's Leader

Copyright © 2005 by John F. Sullivan

iUniverse books may be ordered through booksellers or by contacting:

iUniverse
2021 Pine Lake Road, Suite 100
Lincoln, NE 68512
www.iuniverse.com
1-800-Authors (1-800-288-4677)

ISBN: 0-595-33282-X (Pbk)
ISBN: 0-595-66815-1 (Cloth)

Printed in the United States of America

Dedicated to the memory of my parents
John & Mae Sullivan
Their lives offered daily lessons of credibility, honesty, and integrity

And

To my granddaughter
Lindsay Mae Carroll
Born August 16, 2004
She is the first of a new generation of leaders

Table of Contents

Acknowledgments

Planning to write this book and finally reaching fruition are, as this author quickly discovered, two different things. Without the help of many outstanding people, this would never have been written.

I would like to thank my wife, Theresa, for her patience, understanding, and sharing her insights as to what a good leader is, not only by words, but through example; my children, John and Jennifer, for their encouragement and support throughout my entire career; my personal secretary, Loretta Cirrincione, for her years of commitment to ensuring I did not deviate from the path of true leadership; Bob and Inez Liftig for their keen observations and extraordinary editing skills, without which this book would never have taken an intelligent shape; my close friend and attorney, Robert Saperstein, who has given me many insights on labor/management relationships that have guided me through many difficult times; Reverend Nicholas Anctil and his wife Cyndi for assisting in research and analyzing leadership skills and styles; my friend and colleague, Gene Wolotsky, for providing an excellent model of humanistic leadership; Jerry Spicer, Tom Vasiloff, Chuck Smith, and Craig Kimball, who were dogmatic in insisting that I address this topic; Vincent Perna and Simon Abraham for their assistance with resource material; Dr. Stephen Lando for his loyalty, support and commitment to excellence in leadership and Paul Derkasch Esq. and Kevin Martin Esq. for their counsel on labor matters that impact leadership.

In everyone's life, examples of good and bad leadership are plentiful. In the former category, I must acknowledge my mentor and friend, the late Dr. Robert Young. He first told me the story of the "Old Bull and the Young Bull" and, through his example, showed me what it meant. In the category of exceptional leaders, I must also acknowledge the fine example of honest leadership as practiced on a daily basis by Dr. William Prattella, the chairperson of the Division of Education at Mercy College in Dobbs Ferry, New York. I would also like to thank the staff at iUniverse, Inc. for all of their help, patience, and motivational support, without which, this book would never have been completed.

Finally, I wish to recognize the exceptional dedication of school administrators, supervisors, and teachers throughout the state of New York. They provide our children with living models of leadership, and it is those models that have a profound impact upon all our lives. It is their collective voices that have drowned out the admonitions of poor leaders as they persevere in the service of our nation's youth.

Preface

Webster defines a leader as "someone who is directing, commanding, or a guiding head." Although no value judgment is inherent in this definition, there is an implication that a person who leads is someone special, outstanding, or even god-like. Clearly, a recognized leader is a person who occupies a prominent position in an organization and, by the very nature of that placement, is notable. Beyond that, there is nothing definitive. But, in spite of this, the misuse and overuse of the word "leader" is rampant.

Labels such as "leadoff hitter" or "first chair" imply an elevated level of performance that may or may not be accurate. When names are positioned on an organizational chart, the leader's name is at the top. In a race or in a military charge, the leader is the person out in front. But, listing people in an order does not validate their success or underscore their failure. Descriptive adjectives such as *good* or *great* are earned through an evaluation of a leader's performance. Yet, contemporary society deifies its new leaders upon appointment and then expects their performance to be commensurate with the very productivity that they have allowed the word *leader* to imply. There is something very wrong with this thinking!

In reality, people are frequently thrust into leadership roles without preparation, warning, or a desire to be there. Sometimes, supervisors recognize potential leaders and groom them to lead. But, all too often, vacancies in leadership positions must be filled, and circumstances place unsuspecting souls in unsolicited positions. Then, when appointed, they are expected to perform to the satisfaction of those who have engineered their promotion.

Almost immediately, how people become leaders is far less important than how they function in their new positions. While some accept their new responsibilities with ease, others flounder and fail. In most cases, a new leader's initiation into the world of leadership is more a "baptism by fire" than a product of training. This is how I became a leader and why I wrote this book.

I was twenty-three years old when I began my teaching career in a small public high school in the state of New York. Being the product of a highly disciplined parochial educational system, I found I could not deny my supervisor's request that I become the advisor to two unsuccessful student organizations that experienced faculty members refused to accept appointments to. I was assigned these additional responsibilities and was expected to succeed, despite not having any experience, knowledge, or training in these areas. I discovered that many leaders are *delegated* to positions as opposed to willfully *choosing* them because capable people either cannot be found or will not step forward.

I soon realized that I must "sink or swim" on my own abilities because help in the form of mentoring or meaningful advice was not forthcoming. I researched and solicited information from my colleagues. I listened, especially to those I was advising. I was a collaborator and a shared decision maker without realizing the ramifications of either. Two years later, as a direct result of succeeding in these assignments, I was promoted to Director of Student Activities and principal of the evening Adult Basic Education School. I was twenty-five years old and knew I had the ability to lead.

Two years later, I was promoted again. This time, I became an assistant to the Superintendent of Schools. By then, I knew the leadership style I had developed had a sound philosophical base. I supplemented my practical experience through formal education, earning two master's degrees (Science of Secondary Education and Secondary School Administration) and a Professional Diploma of Advanced Study as a School District Administrator. The more I learned, the more I realized that leadership was an acquired skill. Some leaders might be born, but most are made.

At twenty-eight, I became the youngest public high school principal in the state of New York. I continued to be a successful leader. The skills and techniques I developed in my earlier experiences proved to be applicable in every leadership situation I faced. When I retired after thirty-one years as a high school principal, I had received numerous citations and awards, including "Outstanding Principal of a National Blue Ribbon High School of Excellence." I knew what successful leadership was and how to achieve it.

In 1976, in addition to my principal responsibilities, I became active in professional labor organizations that represent school leaders. I soon held leadership positions in several of them. In 1979, I was elected president of the Regional Association of School Administrators of Westchester & Putnam Counties in the state of New York. I held this position for nineteen years. Concurrently, I was elected treasurer of the New York State Federation of School Administrators, a position I held for seventeen years. I also received national recognition as an elected vice president of the American Federation of School Administrators AFL-CIO. I served for two consecutive terms, totaling six years.

In 1996, I co founded and became the first president of the Empire State Supervisors and Administrators Association of New York State, a position I hold to this day. This organization, with a membership approaching 3,000 school leaders, is among the fastest growing professional associations in the state of New York. When I look back, I realize that, for more than twenty-five years, leaders have chosen me to be their leader and being elected by my peers has been the highlight of my professional career.

In 1998, I became a leadership consultant to both private corporations and public educational institutions. Serving for two years as a consultant vice president of a Wall Street arbitration and mediation firm, I found the same leadership skills that had served me well as a public school administrator served me equally as well in the private sector of business. I knew those skills were applicable to any leadership situation. During the past three years, I again tested my hypothesis as a consultant in three consecutive—but completely different—principalships in three equally difficult public school systems. One dealt with an affluent upper-middle class community; another dealt with a mixed, troubled suburban population; the third was a poor community with an equally as difficult student population. In all three cases, the results were identical. I was able to achieve dramatic measurable positive changes in all aspects of school life.

I know the skills I began to cultivate in 1965 and built upon in subsequent years is precisely what is needed to be a successful leader. Those who consistently apply them will be successful, regardless of the leadership situation. For more than three decades, the application of the principles advanced in this book has enabled me to succeed, and they will help you.

As an adjunct professor of Leadership and Educational Law in the Graduate School of Mercy College in Dobbs Ferry, New York, I have helped many students become successful administrators. The philosophy and skills I taught have been the same for fifteen years and so have been the results. Those who apply the suggestions and principles of *The Common Sense Guide to Leadership* are successful. Leadership is an acquired skill that can be cultivated by anyone who has the desire to do so.

To be successful, a leader must have determination, self-confidence, and a leadership plan. You are determined to succeed; otherwise, you would not be reading this book. You have self-confidence; otherwise, you would not be aspiring to a leadership position. You are already halfway there. The hard part is over. This book will take you the rest of the way. It will bolster your resolve as you implement my suggestions and experience immediate success. It will teach you how to become more organized and how to plan. Success is at your doorstep.

I have arranged this book to be a "quick read" because most leaders are too busy *leading* to get bogged down in minutiae. They prefer to avoid fluff and get to the bottom line. This book is a common sense guide to teach you how to master the art of leadership. It can be read in totality or in segments, based upon your specific needs. It is not a book of philosophical comparisons—though there are some—nor is it riddled with moralistic assumptions. This is a how-to book; it addresses the nuts and bolts of leadership.

When you finish reading *The Common Sense Guide to Leadership*, you will be able to do the following:

- ✓ Know about the qualities and skills you need to be a good leader
- ✓ Focus on what good leadership is
- ✓ Identify your strengths and weaknesses as a leader

If you require a more detailed explanation of any aspect found within these pages, ample reference material is in the bibliography as well as in the numerous research studies that line library shelves. For those who want to be a successful leader or improve upon their existing leadership skills, this is the ideal starting point.

Finally, if you are looking for statistical analysis, convoluted flow charts, field studies, and astrological sign analysis, stop reading right now. This book is not for you. But, if you want common sense applications that will work wonders in achieving leadership success, read on. The information you will acquire from this book—and your resolve to apply it—will form an unbeatable team. Leadership skills are cultivated through determination, study, experience, and hard work. Let's begin.

Foreword

There is a crisis in leadership that is spreading like a plague across our country; those who are most willing to assume leadership roles in our schools, communities, charitable organizations, and politics are frequently those who should be kept farthest away from these responsibilities.

If you can judge anything by the daily newspapers, bankers are embezzling in record numbers. CEOs are ripping off their stockholders. Teachers and religious figures are molesting our children. Politicians elected by the majority are selling out right and left to special interests.

Simultaneously, it is next to impossible to find qualified individuals in many of our communities willing to serve in leadership positions. We have heard all of the reasons: low or no pay, too much personal scrutiny of public lives, the sacrifice of individual leisure time, and the loss of income from more lucrative pursuits.

In some ways, we now have the worst of situations with qualified individuals afraid of public crucifixion sitting on the sidelines while unqualified individuals rise to important positions and disgrace themselves and their institutions. The horrified public then thinks even less of their leaders.

The self-fulfilling dynamics of this conundrum can only increase the velocity of this downward spiral. Honorable individuals will continue to find themselves in trouble; dishonorable ones will steal what they can and—maybe or maybe not—be punished. Committees, clubs, and communities, the glue of the American Republic, will become even more corrupted. The People, about whom all this hoopla is supposed to be about, will continue to abandon their society's future for entertainment.

Moreover, where are the supposedly responsible watchdog groups in all of this? Where are the warning buzzers? The mine canaries? The air raid wardens?

Representatives of the media continue to profit from the public frenzy to enjoy the obvious—that leaders have flaws and their lives are not perfect.

What about the think tanks, the universities, and the schools of management? They have responded to the crisis with ever-growing volumes of administrative flow charts, reorganization proposals, white papers, and behavioral theories distributed exclusively to a rarified audience of the self-anointed.

Meanwhile, the "average people"—the supposed "followers" in our society—are presented with ever more brutal role models (Militant Islam, Saddam, and so forth)

Who can wonder why leadership in this country is in a perilous state of paralysis?

John Sullivan's long-awaited book is directed toward that sidelined category of potential leaders who can still save the day for us, those well-intentioned otherwise qualified individuals who might be willing to step into leadership positions but feel they lack the skills to succeed in the crossfire that meets leadership candidates today.

John Sullivan knows what it is to be a leader because he has been one for more than forty years—one of the small percentage of individuals in our country who have sought and been saddled with a great deal of responsibility at a young age. Moreover, he has founded and continues to lead an impressive array of local, state, and national organizations, often holding similar positions at every level simultaneously.

John not only recognizes our emerging crisis in organizational leadership, but he sees it percolating and permeating throughout our wider society as well. He told me recently that he witnessed an interaction (or a failed interaction) between a father and his son that lies at the core of what most of us know is the root cause of today's leadership crisis—the disintegration of the family unit.

The father was trying to have a serious discussion with his son, who was sitting across the table from him and playing with his portable video game in a neighborhood diner. The father continued speaking to his son for a full hour, and his son continued ignoring him. Without the father's or the son's assertion of leadership, it was apparent there could be no communication. Without that, there could be no interchange, no cooperative effort, or no change in behavior on either part.

The father and son were stalemated—much like the larger American society to which we belong. Clearly, a tragedy is waiting to rush in and fill the vacuum unless we do something about it.

There are cycles in our communal lives as there are in everything and now seems exactly the right moment to hear some of the "old" verities that helped our predecessors respond to challenges at least as serious as those we are facing every day. Perhaps these truisms have gotten lost in all of our electronic shuffle; perhaps they have been buried by the sensationalism and greed in the last decades of the American experiment; perhaps they have even been forgotten.

John Sullivan's book, *The Common Sense Guide to Leadership: Yesterday's Values for Today's Leader*, is a cautionary tale in the spirit of the old "etiquette books" of the nineteenth century that instructed many an immigrant and country rube in how to succeed in the modern American urban and commercial environment.

It is curious that John's book comes at a time when there is spirited debate about the display of the Ten Commandments in public places. Some of those who protest its display—perhaps rightly—argue that presenting the Commandments in public buildings betrays the constitutional injunction against the union of Church and State; others feel they represent a Judeo-Christian that is not held in common with the diversity of today's population. No one, however, has objected to its display because these basic rules no longer apply to the construction and maintenance of an orderly society.

There are times in every nation's history when the tried-and-true lessons that made this country great, need to be remembered and repeated—and this is one of them. We can gas all we want about courage and valor. But, if no one is willing or able to lead the troops, if the army remains huddled around the campfire debating what the "right" thing to do is, and if no one moves, then the battle that must be fought is bound to falter.

Robert A. Liftig, Ed.D.
Westport, Connecticut
August 2004

Introduction

Our parents were our first leaders and our primary role models during the early childhood years when our experiences became the foundation for later emotional and intellectual growth. Many qualities that our parents displayed to us when we were younger are qualities we search for in the leaders we meet throughout our life.

Because of the nurturing qualities we experienced during our developmental years, leaders and leadership became synonymous with something good—like safety, trust, love, security, and so much more. Our parents taught us to believe, trust, and follow other leaders to whom they introduced us. Teachers, clergy, relatives, and family friends played a major role in our emotional development. Collectively, they inhabited a place in which decisions were made in our best interests, and our problems were solved with their leadership. We learned to trust them.

In school, the same qualities were reinforced. Our models of perfection were historical leaders such as the Founding Fathers. We learned George Washington never told a lie and was bravery personified. Thomas Jefferson single-handedly wrote our Declaration of Independence. (We did not know what that meant, but we knew it was good.) Paul Revere rode out courageously to warn an entire fledgling nation. These men were not mere mortals. To us, they were superheroes. The models of perfection our teachers first introduced us to came to life in our history lessons. We thought they were just like our parents, only bigger and better because our parents also paid homage to them.

As we grew older, we grew wiser. Our experiences with leadership broadened. Many of our new leaders did not meet the high standards of those we learned about in our childhood. We began to realize that, although some leaders were honest, competent, and trustworthy, others were not. A certain level of apprehension emerged as the idealism of our early childhood gave way to cynicism and distrust. With each new disappointment, we grew more skeptical. Leadership we once blindly trusted was now suspect. We sensed that our leaders had lost their way. Although well-intended, pressing social issues, fluid moral codes, and pressures to be successful at any cost lowered the ethical bar we believed existed in our younger years. We began to scrutinize everything our leaders said and did. Our leaders became human to us, and they, like everyone else, had flaws.

As we looked closer at the concept of leadership, we realized that it was not easily defined. We learned that today's hero may be tomorrow's fool as leaders strive relentlessly to meet the insatiable and changeable needs of a fickle following. We also realized that fulfilling leadership responsibilities requires patience, sensitivity, and an awareness of one's surroundings. But, the ability to define what it takes to be a good leader still eludes many. However, the answer is actually quite simple. What defines good leadership is a common sense approach to decision making, one that is grounded in a moralistic philosophy that guides us to do the right thing for the right reasons. The pragmatists of this world march to a different drummer. To them, leadership decisions are based upon factors that are more circumstantial than moral. This flawed thinking is the antithesis to the concept of leadership that is presented in this book.

The purpose of *The Common Sense Guide to Leadership* is to help you to focus on the many personal qualities that define successful leadership. Despite moral and ethical differences among leaders, there are several qualities and skills that the successful ones have in common. But, possessing the necessary qualities is only half the equation; applying those to specific roles and circumstances is the other. One, two, or even a dozen traits do not define good leadership. It is how the combination of many human characteristics interact, coupled with historical circumstances that will determine one's success or failure.

For instance, consider leaders like Lincoln, Mussolini, Hitler, Churchill, and MacArthur. They were all successful. They were idealized by millions, could move armies, and destroy lives at will. Yet, they differed significantly in their hopes for their respective countries. Their commonality was that they were all great communicators. Some used this great ability to serve humanity; others used this great ability to destroy it. But, in the final analysis, the worth of a leader is measured not only by the qualities and skills they possess, but how they utilize them.

Despite circumstances that form different expectations for various organizational leaders, there is one universal expectation that all have in common. Leaders are expected to solve problems. Not those little annoying tribulations that are easily addressed and resolved. Anyone can do that. What makes a leader distinctive is the ability to solve big problems; the ones that others cannot. These problems require a special kind of ability, the kind that enables a person to grasp the whole picture and medicate the sickness itself instead of the symptoms. Regardless of style or philosophy, if a leader cannot solve big problems, an organization will eventually select another who can. Possessing basic leadership skills is just the beginning. A leader must be able to put them all together in a way that is productive and, in doing so, demonstrate knowledge, confidence, and determination.

As a leader, you will have an overview of organizational issues that you would not usually obtain as a member. Members in organizations tend to be more concerned about what affects them personally and the impact of specific actions upon their areas of responsibility. If it does not impact them or their areas, the issue is not given much thought. But, for you, it is an entirely different matter. You have an opportunity to analyze all sides of an issue and arrive at a decision that is amicable to all parties. It is your primary responsibility to take decisive actions for the good of the entire organization. The good of the whole must always take precedence over the good of any individual. This is the first of nine (9) assertions upon which this book is based.

1. When one member of an organization wants something that is not in the best interest of the group, the needs of the many must take precedent over the needs of the few. Following this principle is among the more difficult tasks of good leadership. How can situations be resolved for the benefit of the entire organization and not alienate or disenfranchise the dissenting individual or individuals?

2. An organization leader should want to serve in the leadership role. But, as long as a reluctant leader is willing and is capable of fulfilling the responsibilities of the position, lacking eagerness to do so is not in itself a deterrent to being successful. However, the more enthusiastic the leader is to lead, the more enthusiastic the membership will be to follow.

3. Leadership requires different skills that are dependent upon both the specific position and the relationship between the members and the leader. A work-related boss/employee relationship is different than an elected relationship. The authoritarian approach may be very effective in the work place, but it will fail miserably among colleagues who elect you. What works in one arena does not necessarily work in the other. This is why some leaders are not successful when they move from one venue to another, despite a record of outstanding achievement in the prior position. A leader must be flexible. In fact, rigidity is a major reason why leaders fail.

4. It is often difficult to find people to accept leadership responsibilities. In many cases, competent people are just too stressed, too busy, or too frightened to step forward. Sometimes, a leader suffers a loss of income because the time to fulfill the leadership duties reduces the time available to earn more money. This is why leaders of labor, service, or social organizations should derive some benefits other than personal satisfaction for their efforts and why I strongly encourage organizations to compensate leaders for their time. It never ceases to amaze me that many labor-related organizations negotiate for release time and/or financial compensation for leaders

to perform organizational duties (which is a direct cost to the employer), but they frown upon expending funds from their own treasury to compensate that same person. This is flawed thinking. Good leaders should be compensated accordingly.

5. The available field of potential leaders is broad based. Although few may cultivate their inherent leadership abilities, it does not mean that those skills are limited to a small group of individuals. The opposite is true. Yes, some people are much better at it than others. But, given the opportunity and training, leadership skills can be learned. Leadership is an acquired skill. By implementing the recommendations in this book, your ability to lead will improve dramatically.

6. Leaders are selected, either by appointment, election, or benign neglect. But, regardless of how a position is attained, the leader has a primary responsibility to represent the best interest of the members being served. Leaders must be loyal to their constituents. There cannot be confusion or vacillation about this. Members of the organization depend upon their leader to do the right thing for them. This is a trust that should not be taken lightly. In the same way that parents have the responsibility to act in the best interest of their children, leaders must act in the best interest of their members. Leaders and parents share similar responsibilities; this is a sacred trust that should not be abused or taken for granted.

7. Leadership is not for the overly sensitive because it is frequently a thankless job. If a leader is widely recognized for leadership contributions, it is an anomaly. Thus, you must be motivated to unselfishly serve the interests of the organization and must understand your job performance will not necessarily be the criteria upon which you will be evaluated. In fact, the assessment of one's leadership ability is frequently not related to the actual role the leader has played.

   For instance, there was a time when Mussolini was considered to be a great leader. Now, after being reduced to the rank of an incompetent leader, contemporary historians are leading a comeback for him. How about Napoleon? Harry Truman (for example, he was called "Horse's Ass Harry")? Where does the leadership of "Tricky Dick" Nixon or FDR fall on the Richter scale? JFK is now prominent for his leadership standing on two fronts with government taking second place to sexual prowess. It seems that, with the exception of Christ and Moses, everyone else is up for annual review. The evaluation of a leader's performance is forever changing and is frequently not based upon the actual job performance. Leadership is not for the faint of heart.

8. As a leader, self-confidence is absolutely essential. You must believe in your ability to succeed in whatever leadership role you have accepted. If you lack self-confidence, followers will not ascribe to you that which you do not ascribe to yourself. If you want to lead, you must first project the confidence and self-assurance that members want in their leaders.

9. Leadership is leadership. Regardless of the situation, the skills needed to be a successful leader are similar. Although circumstances may cause you to rely on a specific cluster of skills more heavily than another, it is only a matter of degree. For instance, at times, your ability as a public speaker might be more helpful to your organization than your ability to write. Or, perhaps your skill as a mediator may be of greater need. Evolving situations dictate the tools you need to address specific issues. Thus, the more skills you have perfected, the better prepared you will be to lead. Skills are developed through training and experience.

History tells us that leaders come in all shapes and sizes. Some are very good at what they do; others are terrible. Still others are excellent in how they lead, but horrible in what they lead people to do. Clearly, the latter is true of Adolph Hitler and Joseph Stalin. A leader considered to be "great" in one historical period may be perceived as "horrible" in another. Let's consider some historical truisms. Abraham Lincoln was a great leader, or, at least, that is how contemporary historians have memorialized him. On the other hand, as defined by the same historians, Andrew Johnson was a horrible leader. But, in their historical period, many viewed them differently. Thomas Jefferson's star has fallen in recent years because he owned slaves, fathered illegitimate mulatto children, and owed a lot of money. But, less than a hundred years ago, historians classified him as being among the "greats." His evaluation, along with countless others, has become tainted by recently revealed aspects of his personal life that have absolutely no relationship to his leadership decisions.

In an impassioned Floor Speech on Impeachment delivered by Congressman Richard Gephardt to the United States Congress during the President Clinton impeachment hearings (December 19, 1998), he said, "We need to stop destroying imperfect people at the altar of an unobtainable morality." Isn't this exactly what our society does to our leaders? Isn't the risk of public embarrassment for activities in an unrelated lifestyle one of the more significant reasons leaders are refusing to serve?

As historians delve into the personal lives of past heroes, they are discovering imperfections that were not generally known during that leader's tenure. Our heroes had imperfections because they were human. They were men and woman who accomplished extraordinary deeds and were eulogized because they appeared to be superhuman. They had the same needs, dreams, aspirations, hopes, and fears you have. And, despite or perhaps because of their humanity, they did incredible things. Perhaps someday, our society will evolve to a level of sophistication that accepts people for what they are, as opposed to what our insatiable quest for "unobtainable morality" wants them to be.

The Common Sense Guide to Leadership will provide you with a blueprint to succeed…if you are willing to step up to the plate despite the risks that come with all leadership responsibilities. It will help you to develop a leadership style that is based upon those very values that provided you with comfort, warmth, confidence, and security during your developmental years. It will help you to do the right thing, for the right reasons.

The process begins by helping you to analyze and categorize what you already know about leadership and to build upon an existing foundation. The following exercise is an excellent starting point.

The Good and Bad Leader Inventory

Let's begin by tapping into the information about leadership you have already acquired through your own life experiences. Because you have known good and bad leaders, you already possess a wealth of information. You need only a pencil, notepad, and the willingness to take a trip down memory lane.

Think about the good and bad leaders that you have known. In one section of the notepad, list those *negative* experiences you have encountered that have made an impression on you. In a different section, list the *positive* experiences. As an experience is remembered, it should be recorded with the name of the leader to whom the experience relates as well as the approximate time frame. (Identifying the leader helps to separate the real from the vicarious experiences.) This should not be a forced exercise. As a memory enters the consciousness, it should be recorded. Allow this information to accumulate over several days.

When the list has been completed, set it aside for a few days. It should then be revisited, but, this time, focus on the reasons why each listed experience was negative and how that leader could have performed in a more successful way. Next, listing the worst first, rank these experiences. Finally, identify which of these negative patterns you have been guilty of yourself. Taking one at a time, make a commitment to systematically eliminate it from your leadership repertoire. The overall plan is "not to do unto others what has been done to you." Then consider what positive actions you can take to replace the negative ones. This initial exercise is important because it will start you down the path to self-evaluation and improvement.

The information contained in this guide will help you to develop a plan to achieve good leadership patterns. Without a plan to bring about constructive change, people repeat the negative and positive treatment they have personally experienced. This is why abusive parents raise abusive children…who then become abusive parents. People learn by example, and, unless a concerted effort is made to alter a negative behavioral pattern, it will continue. Listing negative leadership experiences is the first step in identifying what you should not become. Listing positive leadership experiences is the first step in making the necessary behavioral changes to become what you want to be. Today, the journey begins.

Chapter 1
The Right Stuff

Organizations frequently set high and unrealistic expectations for their leaders, especially at the state and national levels. They are then shocked to discover that some of their heroes have character flaws that contradict their romanticized vision of leadership perfection. Today's leaders are subjected to the whims of a society that expects one's moral character to be beyond reproach. Although people can intellectually accept the fact that a person with different personal values can lead, they cannot emotionally accept it. Thus, a Gary Hart (who may well have been an excellent national president) failed the litmus test of perfection and never had the opportunity to serve. It is indeed fortunate for America that little was known of the private lives of Alexander Hamilton, Thomas Paine, or John Hancock at the time when they were leaders in the American Revolutionary War. If contemporary standards measured the worth of past leaders, the United States would still be a British colony.

When seeking leaders, organizations are continually looking for "skeleton-less closets." Because this is an oxymoron, many competent people are reluctant to seek or accept leadership positions. They fear those hidden secrets (which we all have but few acknowledge) will emerge and seriously hinder or jeopardize their well-being. Although the criteria for selecting leaders should be simple, they are not. The quest is inhibited because of the underlying expectation that leaders should meet a standard distorted by a false sense of puritanical perfection. It is time to return to the basics!

1. The Leadership Trinity—Credibility, Honesty, Integrity

A leader must possess the qualities of credibility, honesty, and integrity to be successful. These qualities are so interdependent that it is difficult to discern where one begins and another ends. But, without all three, your leadership potential will never be fully actualized. Once you have embraced this Leadership Trinity, your persona will reflect the mores of contemporary society, not the fantasies of a nonexistent one. An organization with unrealistic expectations will inevitably be lead by an unrealistic leader.

Credibility

A credible person is trustworthy and believable. The greater your credibility, the more confident people will be in your organization. People are willing to accept the actions of a credible leader at face value and are more enthusiastic about following the course of action the leader has defined. Credibility in a leader eliminates the need to speculate about a hidden agenda because there is none. Leadership credibility results in universal respect for the organization being led.

Honesty

Honest leaders inspire confidence in their constituents because they are trustworthy. Without honesty, problems cannot be faced and solved, and conflicts cannot be adjudicated for the good of the membership. If you are dishonest, there is limited stability in identifying organizational expectations and goals because the positions and statements attributed to you are forever changing and can never be validated. Dishonesty inhibits the efforts to advance the goals of an organization because the data that is required to make correct assessments is tainted. It is analogous to writing a message in beach sand. What was written may have been correct, but who is to know? The position of the sand has changed, and the actual words have disappeared. Dishonesty breeds distrust and undermines public confidence in your organization.

The dishonest leader becomes a source of embarrassment to the membership. Frequently, dishonest leaders require third-party validation before statements are accepted as being truthful. Simple matters become written contracts. Informal conversations become formal and witnessed by others, and the increased cost of legal services begins to impact organization budgets.

Honesty is not the best policy; it is the only policy. There is no alternative. It is not circumstantial and is not applicable to situations as a pragmatist might deem appropriate. As an honest leader, you will be able to articulate the needs and concerns of your organization without being suspect because the intent of your statements or actions will rarely be questioned. An *honest* leader gives the entire organization *credibility.*

Integrity

The worth of a person is measured by that person's personal code of ethics. A successful leader must have integrity, and one's integrity is partially defined by one's honesty and credibility. As in love and marriage, "You can't have one without the other." And, without integrity, a leader lacks The Right Stuff" to succeed. But integrity consists of much more than being believable, honest, and trustworthy. It also relates to being respectful and sensitive to the needs and concerns of others. Likewise, a person of integrity always keeps personal and organizational commitments. Where some might say that "promises are made to be broken," a person of integrity will say "promises must never be broken."

The message transmitted by the caring leader is one of interest in what others have to offer. Even when confronted with the most outrageous suggestions, a leader of integrity finds ways to help people "save face." A good leader will display confidence in others and freely give assurances to bolster that confidence. A leader with integrity makes members feel emotionally safe because the leader's mannerisms project empathy for the member's well-being. Disagreements never become personal. The focus is always on achieving the goals of the organization.

A leader with integrity is easily recognized and universally trusted. On the contrary, a leader who freely makes commitments for expediency's sake or makes statements that are convenient but not necessarily truthful will soon be discovered to be a charlatan and summarily disregarded. That person's word will become useless and will require reaffirmation and assurances from other trusted individuals before it is accepted.

2. Have Patience

Impatient leaders undermine the shared decision-making process.
—John F. Sullivan

All too often, the leader's timeline is not the organization's timeline for addressing an issue, resolving a problem, or achieving an established goal. Many leaders have been left to flounder because they have gotten so far ahead of their membership on a specific initiative that the membership was unable to follow.

The good nuns of the Sisters of Charity used to say "patience is a virtue." Sister Clementine was right! If a fisherman pulls up his line before the fish has swallowed the hook, the fisherman ends up empty-handed. If the center on a football team snaps the ball to the quarterback before the correct count has been reached, the ball is fumbled, and the play is disrupted. Distributing a statewide standardized test before the designated time will result in test invalidation. A pregnant woman may be anxious for the child to be born, but an earlier delivery would not be in the best interest of the unborn.

Established timelines have a purpose. Disrupting timelines undermines that purpose and often jeopardizes the successful completion of the project. Timelines that are properly constructed and strictly adhered to improve the probability of success.

A Fable:

> Once upon a time, two bulls stood on the top of a hill that overlooked an expansive pasture. The senior of the two bulls was a generation older than the younger one. As they surveyed the pasture, they each noticed a section in the field where many cows were grazing. The always excitable young bull enthusiastically shouted to the old bull, "Let's run down there and jump us a cow!" The old bull responded, "Let's walk down there and jump them all!"

The old bull was patient. Organizations should have goals and realistic timelines for meeting those goals. The established timelines should be mutually agreed upon and mutually amended as necessary. Only under unusual circumstances should a plan that has been rationally and objectively developed be amended.

Timelines should never be changed because of an impatient leader whose judgment might be clouded by the enthusiasm of the moment. History is replete with stories of lost battles because of shots fired too soon. Does anybody love the partygoers who shout "Surprise!" before the honored guest arrives in the darkened room?

Impatience can cause the failure of a well thought out plan. Haste makes waste! But there is another—more subtle—reason impatient leaders should be restrained. An impatient leader makes other people nervous. And nervous people tend to make mistakes. So, in the end, behavior that causes a plan to fail may not necessarily be the action taken by the leader, but an action taken by another person that is caused by the leader's impatience.

Perhaps, the most destructive aspect of an impatient leader is that he or she discourages and undermines the process of shared decision making. People who spend time and energy developing goals and subsequent timelines for implementation are stakeholders and have a vested interest in the end result. Because they are vested, they want to succeed and share in the positive aspects of success. When an impatient leader unilaterally aborts or significantly amends a plan of action, collaborators begin to wonder why they ever became involved in the first place. If that happens often, the list of participants in organizational planning will be greatly reduced and eventually disappear. Even in a paid position, in which people may be forced to participate, enthusiasm will diminish, and the leader will not receive the best efforts of the committee. Stakeholders consider a lack of success to be a personal failure. However, when an impatient leader acts contrary to established timelines and causes that failure, feelings of disappointment are compounded by feelings of anger. An impatient leader will eventually find that they have no one to lead.

3. Get Organized

A disorganized leader causes confusion, disharmony, and discord. Disorganization has many consequences for an organization—none of them good. Fewer things are more frustrating to membership than a leader who is "all over the lot." People do not have confidence or respect for a leader who appears confused, forgets details, is regularly late, misses appointments, or frequently misplaces vital information. Disorganization creates uncertainty. Worse, members tend to replicate a leader's inefficiencies. Over a period of time, a once competently constructed operation becomes as chaotic as its leader.

A major problem of disorganization is that individual members spend more time compensating for the leader's inefficiencies than fulfilling the goals of the organization. A disorganized leader does not give direction to an organization. In addition, more organized members find it frustrating to follow a bungling leader. The task of constantly reminding him or her of relevant matters becomes overwhelming. Disorganized leaders who ignore detail create disorder, and disorder disrupts productivity. Disrupted productivity is costly in time and in resources.

In discussions about a leader's disorganization, someone will inevitably tell the tale of the super leader who had such a cluttered office that no one could find anything. Yet, that leader knew where everything was all the time. The story is usually embellished to include a fictitious secretary who moved some insignificant papers into a different location among the mess, only to have it immediately discovered by that leader.

The leader in this managerial folktale is the closet hero for everyone who champions the right to have a chaotic office. (We all have met at least one of them). They too boast that they can always find anything they need. The problem is that nobody else can. Whenever the leader is absent, organizational work comes to a halt as soon as a vital piece of information is needed or an important item cannot be located. If the leader takes an extended leave, becomes ill, or worse, the organization is thrown into turmoil until someone puts things in their proper order. Behind every chaotic office door is a disorganized leader who will do more harm than good for an organization.

Quick Fixes

The good news is that lack of organization is a correctable evil. Realistically, there is a little bit of disorganization in all of us. The greater the responsibility, the more difficult it becomes to keep track of the organization's business. But there is help available for anyone who is willing to accept it. Keeping and reviewing a daily calendar will help a leader keep appointments and to be on time. Writing down important information and transcribing it into a more permanent location to review at a later time is another easy way to stay on track. To-Do lists are part of most computer programs and are readily available. Technology has invented systems to automatically remind us, minute-by-minute, of tasks that must be completed. Cell phones can ring, watches can buzz, and computers can sing. The world has become a Pavlovian nightmare. If a person forgets what the buzzer or bell is for, the problem is not disorganization. It is dementia.

Beyond bells and whistles, appointing a person as an assistant, secretary, or personal manager has been very successful for those executives who are willing to work on their organizational shortcomings. These are normally trusted companions, employees, or fellow officers who are willing to assist in keeping the leader on task. Whatever it takes to ensure "attention to details" must be done because, without this vigilance, organizational initiatives will fail.

Disorganization that is not corrected translates to unfulfilled goals that negate the need to plan. The end result is an organization traveling a zigzag path to an elusive destination. Substantive issues go unaddressed; others are forgotten. Motivated followers become frustrated by the lack of follow through. Indifferent workers will wait out the leader because they assume their assignment has been forgotten. They rationalize, "How important can a project be if no one follows up on it?" Attention to details is the glue holding the project—and ultimately—the organization together. If pride, fear, or embarrassment prevents leaders from seeking help to correct this problem, that leader will and should be replaced by someone who can provide the organizational skills that a membership requires.

4. Being a Communicator

Webster defines communication as "the exchange of thoughts, messages, or the like by speech, signals, or writing…a system for sending or receiving messages." For the purpose of this section, any variation of the infinitive to communicate refers to exchanging a thought as well as the methods by which this exchange takes place.

As a leader, you must be able to communicate clearly, concisely, and accurately. This is critical for an organization to succeed. The effectiveness of your communication skills is a measurement of your leadership as well as of your organization's ability to articulate its mission and goals.

Becoming a "Good Communicator" is a skill that requires thought, effort, and planning. Two components are critical of precise communication:

First: The communication must *accurately* reflect the *information* that the sender has transmitted.

Second: The message received must be *validated* as being the message transmitted.

Once these issues have been resolved, decisions as to how, when, and to whom information is to be communicated must be resolved.

Accuracy

A message, regardless of how you transmit it, must be precise in both its tone and content. You must take steps, depending on the complexity of the message, to ensure the message says exactly what you intended to say.

Validation

When information is transmitted in any form, a system must be in place to validate its accuracy at both ends of the transmission (i.e., the message sent must be identical to the message received). Remember the old game of telephone? One person whispers a message to another person…who whispers that message to a third person…who whispers that message to a forth person…and so forth down the line. When the final recipient shares the message received with the first sender, it is often distorted or significantly different from the original message. This exercise is used to demonstrate that, unless there are intermediate checkpoints along the way, regardless of the efforts made to construct a clear message, the final recipient may receive a significantly different message than the sender intended.

To validate a message's accuracy, intermediate steps must be put in place to make sure that the sender and the receiver have processed identical information. This can be accomplished through a variety of methods, including verbal and/or written confirmation statements, tape recordings, videotaping, third-party interpretations, and so forth. The greater the importance attributed to the information being transmitted, the greater the need for multiple methods to guarantee accurate transmission and reception.

How?

Once you have established a workable system to transmit and validate a transmission and a determination has been made as to what kinds of organizational information will be transmitted, the next issue to be settled is how the communication is to take place. Because of the large variety of communication formats available, it will be the material and the availability of resources that will determine the means. You should select the method that is the easiest, fastest, and most efficient to yield the desired results. The process can be as informal as a personal conversation, a phone call, or a handwritten note; it can be something elaborate like a videoconference or messenger service. Some information may be better suited to a one-to-one conversation; larger amounts of information may be transmitted via a speech to a large audience, a newsletter, press release, or a massive e-mail. These tools (and many more) are at your fingertips.

The communication process you select is a matter of convenience, personal preference, and leadership style. Once the message has been identified, the audience selected, and the type of the material established (e.g., confidential, classified, and so forth), you will find the method is easily decided.

A leader's failure to communicate information effectively borders on negligence. The proliferation of cell phones has given us all a clear message. People have taken phenomenal steps to be available to receive and transmit information. They want to be kept in the loop and have made the process easy for us to do so. The negative consequences to a leader who fails to communicate are extensive and far-reaching.

To Whom?

Identifying the recipient of information transmitted is a more complicated matter to decide. The decisions as to who should know, who needs to know, and who has a right to know are often convoluted and confusing. For instance, in an organization such as a professional association or a labor union, there are several issues that concern the membership. Much of which should not be revealed, at least not in the time frame that some members would want. A negotiation involving a labor/management contract is a case on point. The membership wants to know what is happening at the table all the time. But sometimes sharing that information can inadvertently reveal a negotiations strategy, upset the membership unnecessarily, or contain information that even the key negotiators have not fully digested. Although members have a right to know, knowing can be counterproductive to achieving an organization's goal. A cardinal rule of leadership is that meeting the goals of the organization must take priority over meeting the individual needs of the membership. Thus, some information may be released on a "need to know" basis, despite an individual's right to know.

During World War II, a common expression heard among military personnel was "Loose lips sink ships." The intended message was loud and clear. There are inherent risks in the indiscriminant release of information of any kind. But, whatever it is and for whatever reason, judgment errors should be made on the side of caution. A cavalier approach to information management can sink an organization's ship.

It is extremely important that you share the organization's communication policy with the membership. Members must know the policy and understand the reasoning behind it. (If these policies are nonexistent, you must develop them.) For instance, matters pertaining to collective bargaining, property purchasing, or strategies to resolve a dispute may well fall into the "do not share" category. Likewise, matters that impact upon an individual member whose particular situation requires confidentiality would fall into the "need to know" category. Although some may make a compelling case to support the membership's right to know, there are times when this type of openness is either disruptive, counterproductive, or an outright threat to an organization's ability to achieve established goals. Helping members to understand the reasoning behind a decision replaces skepticism and suspicion with trust.

As a general rule, even the most confidential pieces of information should be shared with at least one other member in addition to the leader. You should have a confidential backup for critical information if something happens that renders you incapacitated. Unfortunately, tragedy strikes at the most unexpected times. Backup plans should always be in place to ensure a smooth flow of information as well as a continuation of any initiative. There should be a subgroup of members who oversee an organization's day-to-day operations—be it an advisory board, an executive board, or cabinet. Your organization cannot and should not function as a one-person show. The subgroup should identify who should be the recipient of specific information. The decision to share or withhold information should not be a unilateral one.

Sometimes, you must be secretive. When this is the case, the membership must know why. There are also times when you are in possession of information that is not necessarily confidential and is of a general nature regarding the well-being of the organization. Not only does the membership have a right to know, but they have a right to know before it is released to the general public. There is nothing that annoys membership more than hearing information about their organization from an outside source when they should have received the information from within. An organization must have a system in place to efficiently communicate with its members. In today's world of cell phones, phone chains, and e-mails, this is relatively easy to establish.

Policies for sharing information with nonmembers, outside groups, and ancillary organizations should also be developed and regularly reviewed by the membership. Once again, errors made should be on the side of caution. When you are in doubt, information should not be shared, regardless of its relevance, until a policy clarification has been secured.

An added caution is issued when it comes to sharing information with the media. This is a world unto itself and extremely difficult to manage. If an organization must communicate and/or provide information, it should designate one spokesperson that is empowered to speak on behalf of the membership. This spokesperson should be skilled in this particular aspect of the communication process and take direction from the leadership. However, whenever there is a release of information, regardless of the format, the spokesperson must be cautious when entering into an exchange of information with the media. The media can be an organization's greatest friend or worst enemy. This is why there should be only one media spokesperson. An inconsistent release of information can spin an organization in an unintended direction. With one person as the spokesperson, there is less chance of this happening. Public relations and media interaction are fields unto themselves and cannot be fully explored in this book. Those who require assistance in this area should receive it prior to embarking upon any media adventure.

Players and Helpers

There are four major vehicles (players) and two ancillary ones (helpers) in the communication family that an astute leader will heavily utilize. The major players are speech, writing, listening, and kinesics. Their helpers are dress and the Internal Communications Network (ICN).

Speech

Speaking is the most effective way to transmit your message. In recent years, with the development and availability of more sophisticated recording devices, the risk of misinterpreting the spoken word has been greatly diminished. However, there is a difference between the informal speech that takes place in a less structured environment (e.g., the casual dialogue of a small group or one-to-one situation) and the formal speech (e.g., speaker-to-audience relationship) that may involve thousands of people. But, regardless of the manner and structure of the speaking environment, there is a modality that encompasses both the informal and the formal presentation. The guidelines that follow will help you focus on the various components of verbal communication:

✓ You must have a purpose in speaking, and you must know what you are talking about. Having dialogue with an unprepared speaker is a waste of time and energy. It is offensive to the listener and embarrassing to the organization. In many cases, a leader who is ill-prepared to address the topic at hand places the credibility of the entire organization in jeopardy. It is wiser to avoid talking about a topic than to pretend to be knowledgeable in an area in which knowledge is lacking. A speaker who lacks credibility is not an effective leader. The Boy Scout's message for all occasions should not go unheeded. That is, always be prepared! And, if not, prepare to be quiet! Leaders should not be grandstanders who feel threatened if others answer questions that are directed to them. They should never allow ego to replace sound judgment, especially when the organization's credibility is at stake.

✓ You should use words efficiently. The long and cumbersome message is the message that is seldom heard in its entirety. You must present the subject matter in the best format to get the message across clearly, accurately, efficiently, and concisely. Verbose speakers are frequently categorized as blowhards and are not appreciated. Verbosity is confusing, frustrating, and disrespectful to one's time and effort. Many people believe that time is money and that wordiness can be a very expensive commodity. This factor must be given careful consideration when drafting a message, speech, statement, or questions. The more concise the communication, the better it is for the recipient as well as for the speaker.

✓ The vocabulary and syntax you use should be targeted to the ability level of the listener(s). A speaker who uses hundred-dollar words when addressing migrant farm workers should know the message will get lost in the verbiage because the words will be beyond the audience's ability to comprehend them. This distinction may not be so apparent in all situations. Even so, you must analyze what you want to say and find a vocabulary level that is appropriate to all listeners. This may require you to prepare the same message in several ways to address multiple ability levels. You must deliver your message in an understandable format.

✓ When speaking, your physical location in relationship to the audience is extremely important. Listeners prefer to see the person speaking. Whether the speaker stands or sits will depend upon circumstances, but being visible is a necessity. For instance, if you decide to address a large audience from within the audience, prior to speaking, you must study the room to determine the best vantage point from which to speak. You should then speak from that location. You should make eye contact with individuals in the audience regardless of its size. (Many believe that eye contact is a sign of honesty.) You must look for signals from the audience as to how your presentation is being received. If the audience consists of six people and three have fallen asleep and two have gone to the bathroom, the audience is sending you a nonverbal message. Audience demeanor is a good barometer of a speaker's effectiveness. However, in order to make that assessment, your eyes cannot be pouring over notes or looking into the far-off skies.

Regardless of its size, you should be in the path of vision of the audience, and the audience should be visible to you.

✓ Finally, you should never make offensive comments or use inappropriate language. People expect more of their leader. Vulgarity, even though it may initially be well-received, will eventually lower you in the eyes of the people you are leading. Ethnic jokes, sexist terminology, slang, and the like should not be part of your repertoire. You must set an example of appropriate behavior.

Writing

Although speech is the primary method of communication, the written word is a close second. The written statement must be more precise than speech because it is usually not explained by any more detailed information than that contained within the existing text. The written document must stand on its own merits. The writer who is communicating the same information as a speaker has a greater burden to be clear, concise, and accurate because there is either no or limited opportunity for correction or clarification after the fact.

There are several advantages to selecting the written word over the spoken word. The recipient of a written passage can review that passage as often as needed to completely understand its contents. Written documents can be more detailed and technical because the reader can revisit them as often as necessary to assimilate the information contained within. In addition, a reader can select the time and location when the document can be studied without distraction.

This is true regardless of the structure of the written document. A caution is issued here. You must be mindful of a document's permanency. How many letters would never have been written if the writer was mindful of the historical permanency of the written word? Would John Adams, Ben Franklin, or Thomas Jefferson have been as detailed in their writings to companions about their personal life if they knew that, hundreds of years later, their words would be so closely scrutinized?

In this regard, I have a major concern about e-mails. I find that e-mails make it too easy to draft and send written messages. Busy leaders appreciate the conveniences that e-mail offers. I fear that, because e-mails are so easy to construct and send, too many messages are sent in haste and not given much consideration. Poorly constructed or not rationally thought out e-mails will come back to haunt you. The cautions that follow apply to all forms of written communications.

The writer must be correct in the information being provided, and it must be written at the comprehension level of all recipient(s) to whom it is being directed. It must also be appropriate in its presentation. You must always remember its permanency. The selected format for the written message is circumstantial, but it must be properly prepared and correct in its subject matter and syntax. Whether it is a one-page letter or a one hundred-page journal, your goal must be perfection in content and form. It will be there long after you are not.

Most written documents have an established and generally acceptable format. For instance, there is an established design for a personal letter that is part of every elementary school writing program across the entire country. Corporations have specific formats for a memo that differs from that of an annual report. Giving a written document a specific structure adds to its clarity and frequently telegraphs its purpose. It also provides a higher level of consistency throughout the entire organization. It is vital upon the part of the writer to utilize established and generally accepted formats. Where they do not exist, you must introduce them. Information about these formats is listed in the bibliography or can be found in the writing sections of any good bookstore or library.

Listening

Good listening is an element of good communications. A good leader talks twenty percent of the time and listens the other eighty percent. Unfortunately, some leaders (especially neophytes) equate winning an election or securing a promotion with being the equivalent of deification and infallibility. They choose to speak more and listen less. This is a mistake.

An attentive listener communicates a message of interest in what the speaker is saying. It also tells the speaker his views are valued. However, interrupting a speaker for reasons other than for clarification conveys an entirely different message—one of disinterest. A speaker never appreciates a conversation that is interrupted by visitors, phone calls, hand messages, and so forth. The more successful you are at avoiding interruptions, the greater the probability of clarity and understanding. An uninterrupted message is more easily heard and processed.

A listener who uses the "kill the messenger" approach inhibits dialogue. You must be receptive to the speaker and avoid being argumentative. Comments such as "Just tell him what he wants to hear" or "She will really get annoyed if you tell her that" are very strong indicators that you are really not a true listener. When this happens, valuable resources are cut off, and the free flow of information is jeopardized. Fear and futility replace admiration, respect, and support.

When someone is speaking to you, you should avoid judgmental interjections because they inhibit conversation. Once the message has been transmitted in its entirety, it should be summarized if clarification is needed. It is critical for good communication that all parties involved in the process understand and agree upon exactly what has been said. Depending upon the context, some commentary may be necessary, or some assurances may be required. But, if a plan of action is to be developed because of a conversation, then that plan should be constructed only after the entire message has been completed and understood. Efforts to develop an action plan in the middle of hearing the problem could result in the loss of unspoken—but necessary—details that are needed for complete understanding. Worse, it could result in an inadequate action plan.

It is essential to the communication process that, when a question is asked, the respondent understands the question before answering. Sometimes, it is helpful to learn the motivation and intent of the question before responding. There is a lesson on point that can be learned from the personal experience of poor Sally Miller.

A Story

Sally Miller was married to Freddy for sixty years when he passed away. Sally had been so dependent on Freddy for everything that she could not live without him. So, she decided to take her own life. She went to the basement and retrieved Freddy's old World War II revolver, but, because Sally did not want to make a mess with an unsuccessful suicide attempt, she called her doctor and asked the question, "Dr. Jones, exactly where is the heart of a woman located?" Dr. Jones responded, "The heart of a woman is located just below a woman's left breast." That evening, Sally shot herself in her left kneecap.

This is an example of a serious breakdown in communications!

There is a difference between listening and hearing! Dr. Jones did not understand the question, and Sally did not understand the answer. When answering a question, you must understand it in its entirety before responding.

Regrettably, personal contact is becoming a lost art. Faxes, e-mails, general bulletins, written directives, and so forth are all ways that leaders communicate without interacting with the people with whom the communication is being conducted. But, these tools are not acceptable substitutes for direct, personal interaction. The willingness of leaders to sit down and talk one-to-one is still the best motivator and should be utilized whenever there is an opportunity to do so.

Listening entails more than giving a speaker your undivided attention. You must listen with your *instincts* as well as your ears. A component of listening is being aware of messages the speaker is sending through voice patterns and inflections because these aspects of speech sometimes speak volumes. For instance, if the voice inflection does not match the message, something is wrong or, at least, not being interpreted correctly. For good listening to take place, the recipient must decipher what is being said from *what is really being said.* How often has a hysterical child responded to the question, "What's wrong?" with one word, "Nothing." Clearly, the words spoken are in conflict with the intended message of the crying child. A critical component of good listening is keen observation.

Finally, to be a good listener, you must be accessible. How often do responses to the question, "Why didn't you tell me?" result in answers such as "I couldn't reach or find you," "Your secretary said you were not available," or "You're never around!" Good listening begins with availability, requires attentiveness, and demands observation.

Kinesics: Messages from the Body

Often forgotten, but always present, are the nonverbal messages transmitted by our bodies. The interpretations of body movements can (at times) provide greater insight as to what the speaker is really saying than the actual words being spoken. Do not overlook the powerful messages that bodies send through gestures, facial expressions, hand movements, and the like. Sometimes, these movements are planned and controlled. At other times, they are reflexive and very difficult to contain. For instance, fear or happiness is reflected by the body in ways that are difficult to suppress. Twitches, sweating, trembling, and so forth are all part of this process. Bookstores and library shelves are lined with volumes of research that demonstrate that a person's inner thoughts are revealed through body language (i.e., kinesics). Sometimes, the body sends a message that contradicts the words being spoken. Astute leaders attempt to manipulate their body movements to support the messages they want listeners to believe in.

Charlie Chaplin was the master of nonverbal communication. Without uttering a sound, his audience knew exactly what was on his mind. A mime carries nonverbal communication to the extreme. "Jury watchers" are constantly seeking clues as to how a juror is leaning by analyzing that juror's body movements. Recently, the juror in the Tyco embezzlement trial said a mouthful without saying a word. The end result of her hand gestures was the declaration of a mistrial.

You must be in tune with your body in order to ensure the message your body is transmitting is in agreement with the message you intend to send. This is a particular problem for politicians because the media analyzes their body movements to find either support or contradictions for the words they are speaking. Honesty is the best policy. If for no other reason, the body might tell an observer what the speaker is really thinking. In the same way that you must analyze speeches and writings, you must also pay attention to kinesics—yours as well as others.

The processes of speech, writing, listening, and kinesics working together form a powerful cluster of communication tools. When all these components are in sync, it is difficult for a message to be misunderstood. Some leaders speak, some write, and others gesture. In larger organizations, an even greater variety of tools are available to get the message across. Press agents and public relations departments abound for this very purpose.

Related to a system of communication but ancillary to the players (speech, writing, listening, and kinesics) are two helpers: dress (the uniform) and the Informal Communications Network (ICN).

Dress (The Uniform)

In the mid-1970s, John T. Molloy wrote a book entitled *Dress for Success.* Molloy made a compelling argument that there is a strong connection between one's clothing and one's acceptance into specific work and social environments. He believed that one's clothing was an additional vehicle for communication. Since its publication, research has consistently supported the validity of this concept. In fact, researchers have even identified power colors and power ties to establish moods such as dominance, subservience, and the like. Clothing is a major contributor to the communication process.

The worldwide garment industry has invested billions of dollars in advertising men's and women's apparel. The message is always the same; the listener/reader/viewer will be more successful in business relationships, love, sporting activities, and so forth if he or she dresses in a particular way. Despite what some might consider foolish or distasteful, there are significant social reasons why teenagers insist on wearing designer clothing and to dress as their friends do.

Clothing reflects your communal and professional position as well as your level of social sophistication, interests, and personal wealth. Some outfits send messages of affluence; others send messages of poverty or rejection. There are times when the message a leader is transmitting confuses members because the words are saying "I'm in charge," but the clothing is saying, "Can you help me out? I can't afford a cup of coffee." Dress is another tool in the leadership toolbox to help establish clear and concise communication, and it should be utilized as such.

The United States Constitution protects your right to dress as you please as a component of its First Amendment. Dress is considered to be a form of free speech. It cannot be taken away or restricted unless there are extenuating circumstances that justify restricting it. For instance, a child's right to wear a T-shirt to school with almost any message or symbol on it is protected. But, one of those symbols cannot be a swastika because that symbol represents a threat to public safety and can be prohibited. However, in most cases, dress is a form of speech that cannot be restricted.

In public institutions where dress codes have been instituted, the Supreme Court has struck them down as being unconstitutional, that is, a civil rights violation. Public school children, for example, cannot be required to wear a school uniform even for physical education classes because it interferes with a child's right to freely express him or herself. The government recognizes that dress is a communicator, a form of speech that is protected under the Bill of Rights. In a sense, dress is speech.

The astute leader uses clothing as an additional opportunity to communicate and bolster his or her leadership role. Imagine attending a funeral service in which the pallbearers are wearing bright red sports jackets, white scarves, tan pants, and black sneakers. Clearly, this would be shocking because one would expect an outfit that properly reflects the seriousness of the occasion. In fact, this type of dress would be offensive and disrespectful. A black suit and tie would be more appropriate. An outfit frames the purpose of a gathering. As the leader, you are expected to maintain a certain image. Dressing appropriately becomes an additional means of projecting and maintaining that image.

You should dress for the leadership position you occupy, regardless of or in spite of how others may choose to adorn themselves. Dress sends a message to members and nonmembers alike. Like kinesics, it is another form of silent speech.

The Informal Communications Network (ICN)

You must be current on all issues that are relevant to the well-being of the organization. You are expected to keep a finger on the pulse of the organization 24/7. You must be "hyper-vigilant." There is no acceptable excuse for not knowing, at least, not in the eyes of the general membership.

In reality, there will always be situations about which you are unaware. The larger an organization, the greater the possibility exists that previously unknown information from an outside source will surprise or blindside you. To minimize this risk, you must put a system in place to reduce or eliminate these unpleasant surprises. One of the more successful approaches to accomplishing this objective is to construct an Informal Communication Network (ICN). If constructed properly, you will always be in the loop and current on organizational matters.

The goal of an ICN is to develop an informal team that filters necessary information to you without being bogged down by rank and protocol. Depending upon the specific needs, size, and purpose of your organization, an ICN might include representatives of the various organizational components within the operational power structure as well as members of those informal groups that help an organization run smoothly.

In most organizations, the least likely people always seem to be in possession of the most important information. They may or may not be a part of the power structure, but they are nonetheless an intricate part of the operation. In a corporate structure, they may be custodians, mail room clerks, or interns. In a club or professional association, they may be relatives or business associates from outside the group. These information magnets are always present and can be an invaluable resource to keeping you up to speed on all organizational matters.

Briefings, written or verbal reports, verbal exchanges at morning role call, coffee klatches, or water cooler chitchat are all invaluable sources of information. The goal is for you to include people in an informal structure who know what you need to know and are willing to share it. These people do not need to be connected to each other as long as they are connected to you. Information can be transmitted by word of mouth, e-mails, phone calls, or smoke signals; the method does not matter. What does matter is a flow of current and accurate information. As an added benefit, this type of informal system enables you to demonstrate a willingness to communicate and an availability to do so.

The larger the organization, the more complex the ICN will be. But, as complex as it may become, it must remain separate from the normal and frequently formal network that exists in most established organizations. In fact, the ICN can serve as a validation system for information that is processed through formal channels.

The nonnegotiable goal of every organization should be flawless communication at every level, all the time. You should never be surprised by receiving information that comes from sources outside the established structure when it should have already been communicated from within. The failure of a communication system to operate successfully could result in a major breakdown within the organization. Therefore, it must be monitored and improved as circumstances dictate. The ICN will help you to accomplish this.

5. Decisions…*and developing a thick skin*

Leadership is making decisions; it is what you are expected to do. How you arrive at a specific decision is a matter of personal style. Do you act unilaterally? Do you collaborate? What about a majority vote? Regardless of style or the method chosen, you must make decisions and assume responsibility for those decisions. It is a primary responsibility of the job.

The social psychologist Abraham Maslow placed acceptance and self-esteem at the very top of his hierarchy of human needs. He taught that, above all, people want and need to be loved, praised, adored, and recognized for their contributions. This human need ranks second only to survival. But, if a leader does not manage this need, it can be a significant inhibitor to making any difficult or controversial decisions. The fear of being criticized can immobilize a leader to the point where he or she is unable to decide at all. But, decision making and leadership are one and the same. If there is no decision maker, there is no leader. If your fear of criticism or failure is so great that you are unable to make decisions, you must be replaced by someone who is better able to deal with it.

General Colin Powell puts it very clearly when he speaks of leaders who are too sensitive of criticism. He says:

> Being responsible sometimes means pissing people off. Good leadership involves responsibility to the welfare of the group, which means that some people will get angry at your actions and decisions. It's inevitable if you are honorable. Trying to get everyone to like you is a sign of mediocrity; you'll avoid the tough decisions, you'll avoid confronting the people who need to be confronted, and you will avoid offering differential rewards based on differential performances because some people might get upset. Ironically, by procrastinating on the difficult choices, by trying not to get anyone mad, and by treating everyone equally "nicely" regardless of their contributions, you simply ensure that the only people you'll wind up angering are the most creative and productive people in the organization.

A perfect example of what General Powell meant was found recently in a small unnamed public school district. In that school district, there are two elementary schools that accurately reflect the makeup of the community. They are as homogeneous as schools can be. The grade levels (one through five) are the same, the class sizes and staffing are about the same, and there is no significant difference between the schools in regard to family wealth, education, family background, race, religion, and so forth. The teaching staffs and ancillary services are also comparable. Yet, one school, year after year, significantly outscores the other one on national and state test scores. However, when the scores are reported to the public, the superintendent of schools lumps the scores of both schools together and reports the average. Recently, when the superior school protested its lack of recognition year after year, the superintendent stated that he could not single out any one school for recognition. This decision may have been expedient and politically sensitive to the concerns of the less successful school staff, but it offended and discouraged the superior one. That staff believed (and rightfully so) their efforts were being used to cover up deficiencies in another building and they were not receiving the recognition they deserved. This is perfect example of a leader who, by trying not to get anyone mad and treating everyone equally "nicely" regardless of their contributions, simply ensures that the only people that he winds up angering are the most creative and productive people in the organization.

Leadership is decision making; decision making generates heat. Harry Truman said it best, "Those who can't stand the heat should stay out of the kitchen."

6. Having "Administrative Rhythm"

Timing is often the difference between success and failure. Administrative rhythm is being in step with the administrative environment, knowing what to do, and when to do it.

The actor Richard Gere has strong convictions about world peace and forgiveness for mankind's shortcomings. Who could disagree with him? In fact, most of the time, his beliefs are respected, accepted, and even applauded. Unfortunately, he attempted to articulate them at a rally held in New York City shortly after 9/11 that had been organized for the stated purpose of assisting the families of victims of that attack. He was almost tarred and feathered by an audience that was not in the right frame of mind to think about forgiveness for the people who had killed their friends and loved ones. Good idea…bad timing! Richard was out of sync with his audience. The end result was that his message fell on deaf ears. In fact, instead of making people more peaceful, he made them angrier. Clearly, he had chosen the wrong time and the wrong place. He lacked administrative rhythm.

To be a successful leader, you must have a sense of timing. Like a great race car driver, baseball hitter, quarterback, or gymnast, success depends upon timing. Poor timing usually translates into poor results. Sometimes, you must wait for an organization to catch up before advancing new ideas. There are other times when an idea is not fully understood until other components are implemented. A great idea for tomorrow could fall on deaf ears today. "When one is up to his ass in alligators, it is sometimes impossible to keep in mind that the primary objective of the mission was to drain the swamp." A leader with poor timing is like the proverbial bull in a china shop. The leader with a propensity for saying the right thing at the wrong time would be better off not speaking. The mission is always to advance the goals of the organization. Every action you take must be evaluated for its timeliness as well as its intended outcome.

Taking actions or speaking on issues that are counterproductive to meeting organizational goals is not good leadership. The process of implementing a decision in a timely fashion is sometimes more important than actually making it. If you lack administrative rhythm, you are missing a key ingredient for a successful administration. Some decisions require no thinking at all. The time flows naturally as circumstances dictate. But, other issues are more complex and require finesse and manipulation.

Generally, when considering taking an action, the timing of its actualization is the first issue for you to consider. When in doubt about the correct timing, you should err on the side of caution and wait until it is more appropriate to do so. That is administrative rhythm.

7. Holding and Folding

Take a lesson from Kenny Roger's "The Gambler." There will be times when, regardless of the outcome that you want as a result of taking a specific action, it is just not going to happen. Remember the childhood rhyme, "He who fights and runs away lives to fight another day." Some battles will never be won, some will be easily won, and others might be winnable at another time. Time is always better expended on projects that are more likely to succeed than those that never will.

Unfortunately, some leaders let their ego get in the way of sound judgment. To them, every issue becomes a personal one. Big or small, important or unimportant, they must win at any cost. At some point, this type of leader becomes too much of a liability for the organization. A leader needs to pick the right issues to battle over. Whether the impetus comes from within or outside the organization, there are times when, regardless of the merits of a case, it is time to fold.

You cannot behave or make decisions based upon emotions. You are expected to remain, cool, calm, and objective at all times. It comes with the territory. You are held to a higher standard of behavior. Over the long run, if you act on your emotions as opposed to your intellect, you will be criticized by your membership for doing so. No one really likes to see the team's manager or coach ejected from a game for allowing uncontrolled emotions to result in poor behavior. Players yes…managers no! The reason breaks down to rationality versus irrationality. Even the most unreasonable members depend upon their leader to act rationally.

At some point, you will be blinded to a given issue's merits. When this happens, you must remember the good of the organization is the most important concern. The leader must recognize this personal vulnerability and take the necessary steps to protect the organization against it. It happens to everyone at some time or another. However, when this happens, it is essential you yield the decision on that particular matter to the membership at large, a committee, or a more objective fellow officer to determine the final course of action. Stubbornness under the guise of principle is a disservice to the membership. A good leader always seeks the best decision for the organization, maintains objectivity, and picks winnable battles. Know when to hold and when to fold.

8. Empower and Shield

An effective leader recognizes others' leadership potential and capitalizes on that potential. Through the process of empowerment, a leader assigns responsibilities to another person(s) who has been authorized to act on behalf of the organization. However, once empowered, a leader must shield a member against recriminations in the event the juxtaposition of authority results in the failure of the mission.

Empowerment

Implicit in empowering a member to act on behalf of the organization is your responsibility to support that person. Without support, there is no empowerment. How many times have you heard someone say, "Just a minute, I'm only one person," "I can't do it all," or "Wait your turn, I've only got two hands"? Excuses like these are used to justify inefficiency and poor productivity. This lack of productivity is generally caused by leaders who are so controlling that no decision can be made or any action taken without their own personal imprimaturs. These leaders are either unable or unwilling to empower membership.

To empower is to deputize, authorize, and help a member complete a specific assignment. The empowered member cannot be overly supervised. Restrictive supervision reduces the member to that of a glorified messenger who lacks the authority to act independently. This is micromanagement and is the death knell for empowerment. Leaders who micromanage are incapable of empowering anyone. By their actions, they are telling their membership they are insecure in their roles as leader and they lack confidence in those around them. This style of leadership is an extension of the "If you want something done right, do it yourself" self-aggrandizing school of management. These leaders see their inability to relinquish any authority, that is, their need to micromanage, as a strength that is often confused with dedication. In reality, it is a crippling weakness.

Micromanagers strip members of the ability to achieve the goals they were assigned to meet. They disenfranchise those who are willing and able to serve. Their system is inefficient, cumbersome, and undermining. It results in a duplication of efforts, squanders valuable time, and discourages volunteerism.

The cornucopia of people capable of being empowered is extensive. Many individuals have the ability to lead if given the opportunity and the training to do so. Leadership is an acquired skill. The larger the organization is, the greater the need and opportunity for leaders to empower membership by sharing responsibilities.

Shield

A member who has been empowered to act on behalf of an organization must be afforded some degree of protection from the negative consequences of a failed assignment. You must provide that shield. Otherwise, the risk of failure to an empowered member will greatly outweigh the benefits derived from success. The end result will be the refusal of members to accept an assignment. The decision-making process will be inhibited to the extent that empowerment becomes ineffective.

Leaders are driven by a desire to succeed. Failure is the antitheses of success and, therefore, unacceptable. The contemporary version of "To err is human; to forgive is divine" is "FUHGEDOABOUDIT!" Either way, it is easier said than done. A failed initiative is a matter of great concern and rightfully so. However, the greater concern is how the leader addresses it.

Pencils have erasers, computers have spell checks, and leaders have scapegoats. The latter is odious to the hypothesis of empowerment and shared decision making. If a leader does not share recognition for organizational successes and does not accept responsibility for organizational failures, the leadership team will inevitably be reduced to a unit of one. If empowered members are expected to make decisions, they must be secure in knowing they can make mistakes without recriminations, especially by the leader.

If a person takes a multiple choice test and answers ninety-eight out of one hundred questions correctly, that person's test performance would receive an excellent grade. Yet, two mistakes were made. If making two mistakes jeopardizes one's reputation or status, that person will avoid being tested ever again.

People do not deliberately fail. Competent leaders empower capable members. But, failure happens. While you are disappointed, the member responsible for the failure also suffers. That person has failed on two levels—by not meeting your expectations and by hindering the organization's progress. It does not serve any useful purpose to humiliate, embarrass, or ridicule a person who has not successfully completed an assignment. On the contrary, this type of reproach will result in grave consequences for both the organization and its leader.

When an initiative fails, the best advice to follow can be found in the words of a popular song by the late Frank Sinatra, "Just pick yourself up, and get back in the race." This is your only reasonable course of action. Certainly, efforts must be made to correct errors, but the human aspect cannot be overlooked. It is during these times that your true worth is tested. You must assume responsibility for the failure, protect the integrity of the member, investigate the reasons for the failure, and take corrective steps to prevent a recurrence…and then move on to other organizational matters. This is empowerment and shield. Both are necessary if you are to capitalize on the skills of membership.

Leaders who get stuck in the quagmire of yesterday's failures never address tomorrow's concerns. Brooding over a failed operation causes a paralysis that cripples the entire organization. FUHGEDOABOUDIT!

9. Secretive and Confidential

"You'll always be my best friend, you know too much."

—*Anonymous*

There is a significant difference between being secretive and being confidential. A secretive person is someone who conceals thoughts from others, that is, a person who keeps information about a variety of topics very guarded. On the other hand, a confidential person is someone that others tend to entrust with private or secret matters. A good leader must be both secretive and confidential. Somewhere between the paranoia of J.R. Ewing and the naïveté of Mother Teresa, a proper balance exists between what information can and cannot be shared, when confidences should be maintained, and when they should be broken.

Secretive

A decision to be secretive is a component of judgmental leadership. What types of information you should or should not be secretive about is a constant struggle faced by all who hold responsible positions. However, leadership does not mean giving up your right to a private life, your right to have private thoughts, or your right to maintain private relationships and confidences. Being secretive is often a matter of personal discretion. In fact, when information of a sensitive nature that does not have to be revealed is, it creates problems that may never have surfaced if the information had been kept private. For instance, discussing matters that cause another person to needlessly worry or expressing personal dislikes are of no real benefit to an organization unless talking about them serves a purpose in advancing, supporting, or protecting the membership. Many leaders are too free with information that should not be shared.

In America, we say, "What goes around comes around." In Italy, they say "Don't spit in the air; it's liable to come down and hit you in the eye." I am sure that all cultures have similar expressions to transmit the same warning. Be careful what you say and how you say it because it can come back to haunt you. You must be cautious about the personal and organizational information you decide to share.

Leadership can be a lonely position. Sometimes, not being able to speak freely about normal fears and insecurities will frustrate you. But, a constant sharing of insecurities causes a level of anxiety that can negatively impact an entire organization. Likewise, you are sometimes in possession of information that should not be shared because it might be destructive to the organization or its members—even if you find that information to be personally upsetting. The range of possibilities is enormous. There are many circumstances when specific secretive information should only be revealed on a "need to know" basis. You must exercise sound judgment when dealing with sensitive information of any kind. Errors should be made on the side of caution. As leader, you must be secretive.

Confidential

Being confidential is another matter. All parties to a confidential conversation or the recipients of a confidential document must be told before any sensitive information is exchanged that it might not be possible for you to keep whatever transpires, in whatever form, confidential. It is not possible to give anyone an irrevocable guarantee the confidence will not be broken, even if all parties agree to keep it. For instance, if subpoenaed in a judicial proceeding and placed under oath, most confidences are not protected under law. If fact, a person can be forced to reveal the contents of a conversation or document under penalty of law or suffer grave consequences for not doing so.

The law does protect certain confidences. Confidential conversations between a doctor and patient, attorney and client, or priest and confessor fall into this category. But, most other confidences are not protected, and sharing parties must depend upon the nature of the confidence, the circumstances surrounding it, the integrity of those involved, and the judgment of the leader.

Before you engage in a confidential conversation, you must establish ground rules. If you are uncertain the confidence can be kept, the other party should be informed of that possibility before you exchange sensitive information. It should also be clearly understood that information that is illegal or detrimental to the health and safety of another person or the organization cannot remain confidential.

Personal information about a person is a perfect case on point. People are not entitled to receive confidential information simply because they are curious or are related to a party to whom the confidence is about. In fact, federal law determines a person's right to privacy and another's right to know. Grave consequences exist for anyone who violates them. For instance, parents who pay a fortune in college tuition are often surprised and frequently infuriated to learn that, even though they are paying the bills, they cannot review their child's college transcripts without the child's permission.

Privacy is a treasured possession of a free society, and, within the framework of that free society, the right to receiving, sharing, or protecting confidential information is paramount. For this reason alone, when dealing with confidential information, people who need to know must demonstrate to you—beyond a reasonable doubt—that they are actually entitled to the information in question.

When releasing confidential material to anyone, you must have a valid reason for doing so. If you are to be approachable by the membership, you must be secretive and confidential. But, to be either is not always an easy determination to make. For instance, sharing confidential information about a key employee's pregnancy might be necessary only when not sharing it at that time would be detrimental to the organization's needs. On the other hand, it might be absolutely necessary to share confidential information (e.g., a key employee is taking a job at a competitor's firm) if informing others is critical to protecting the organization, regardless of how the leader learned of the news. But, because of the endless numbers of circumstances when a confidence might be broken, it is not prudent to blindly give assurances that it will be kept.

When someone invites you to participate in a confidential conversation or review confidential documents or the like, you must declare up front that the confidence will be kept only if it is possible to do so. As a general rule, secrets should not be revealed indiscriminately or confidences broken unless it is absolutely necessary to do so.

It is not helpful to an organization for its leader to be thought of as a gossip or someone who cannot be trusted with sensitive information. Leaders walk a very fine line in this area, and those who use poor judgment in handling information will eventually relinquish their leadership positions to someone who is better able to handle it.

10. Risk Taking

"If you ask enough people for permission, you inevitably come up against someone who believes his job is to say, 'No,' so the moral is, don't ask."
—General Colin Powell

Sometimes, it is better if you seek forgiveness after an action has been taken than to request permission before it. There are times when it is not possible, practical, or feasible to reconvene a governing body to make decisions on a particular initiative or a course of action before it takes place. Likewise, only a weak leader seeks organizational clarification each time the wind changes direction. You are expected to make decisions, exercise common sense, and carry out the membership's intentions. Good leaders are risk takers.

Despite extensive planning, no one can anticipate every variable. Circumstances change, people change, and goals change. An essential tool of sound leadership is flexibility. You must plan for the unexpected and react accordingly. Opportunity as well as trouble frequently knocks without warning. There are times when an unanticipated development presents a favorable opportunity to serve the interests of an organization. It might be the acceptance of a contract, the purchase of property, or the hiring of a staff member. Knowing this possibility would be lost if not acted upon and not being able to get prior membership approval, a good leader takes the risk and acts. Carpe diem!

When organizations establish goals, some inevitably have higher priority than others. However, you are expected to pursue every goal, either personally or through intermediaries who have been empowered to act on your behalf. Sometimes, circumstances require you to make unilateral decisions that impact a plan, a timeline, or both. You are expected to exercise initiative and sound judgment. You are expected to be a decision maker.

There are many reasons and circumstances when it is necessary for you to take a risk and decide to follow a particular course of action. When circumstances develop that require you to take a risk, the following guidelines will help you:

- ✓ The Risk must fall within the authority level of the risk taker.
- ✓ The Risk must serve the best interests of the organization.
- ✓ The Risk must fall within the parameters of achieving established goals.
- ✓ The Risk must have a high probability of success and a limited downside.
- ✓ The benefits of taking the Risk must be readily apparent as well as the consequences of an unsuccessful effort.
- ✓ The benefits of success must always outweigh the consequences of failure.
- ✓ The Risk must be within the confines of the law.

For instance, in the process of protracted labor negotiations, the governing body of a labor organization decides that, if the contract is not settled by 11:45 PM, the leader is to call for a general membership strike. But, at 11:00 PM, the leader believes that substantial progress is being made and a settlement will be reached within the next six hours. The leader exercises good judgment, takes a risk, and postpones the strike despite the expectations of the governing body to do otherwise.

When measuring this decision against the criteria for risk taking, the leader determined that, not only was the decision to postpone a job action in the best interest of the membership, it was also within his authority to do so. The benefits of taking the risk greatly outnumbered the consequences of failure, and a bad decision would have had a limited downside. There was more to gain than lose by forestalling a strike. It was an appropriate risk to take.

Every initiative has an anticipated outcome. It is the responsibility of the leader to work towards meeting the organizational goal. A leader who constantly tests the waters before making a decision may keep the position, but he or she is not a true leader. Leaders are expected to think outside the box and make decisions for the good of the organization—and sometimes making a decision requires taking a chance.

Good leaders know how their organizations will decide on most issues. They know the intent of the membership. This does not mean that a hypothetical vote would always be unanimous in favor of how a leader believed the membership would have decided. But, it does mean that, if the action would not have been approved, the actual vote would have been very close. Certainly, on occasion and over a period of time, a leader can misjudge his or her constituents. But anything more than a few misses means that the leader is out of touch and should consider stepping down or become more actively involved in analyzing and addressing organizational needs.

11. Recognizing the Contributions of Others

A good leader acknowledges and positively reinforces the membership's efforts and contributions to the organization. Those individuals or committees who have been delegated to and have successfully fulfilled the responsibilities of an assignment should be recognized for their achievement. A good leader not only acknowledges the contributions of others, but he or she also provides positive reinforcement to ensure their continued efforts. As a general rule, good leaders assume the responsibility of failed efforts and share the limelight with others when accomplishments are noteworthy. Positive recognition and praise for contributions to an organization are powerful aphrodisiacs that will inspire the membership at large to continue or even accelerate their contributions.

From the time a child is potty trained, applause and cheers of joy accompany accomplishments. Community service organizations such as the Lions Club or the Kiwanis Club begin each meeting praising members for personal or organizational accomplishments. Athletic teams—both amateur and professional—utilize cheerleaders to lead the admiring crowds in shouting chants of praise for players on their team. The purpose of these cheers is to inspire the team to work harder for victory. Corporate America uses bonuses, Little League uses trophies, and schools use medals to recognize achievement.

Social self-help groups such as Weight Watchers cheer in unison for every member who has successfully lost even an insignificant amount of weight. This has become an expectation when one joins a support group. And, isn't the new trend in child discipline to recognize and praise positive behavior and ignore anti-social behavior? Research demonstrates, time and time again, that people can be trained to do almost anything if they are praised for doing so. As frightening as it is, there are even parents in this world who bask in the praise they hope to receive for sending their own child to commit suicide and, in the process, kill hundreds of defenseless people in crowded shopping malls.

It is an irrefutable fact that people improve productivity when they receive positive reinforcement. Recognizing a person's efforts, even if those efforts are for negative acts, will cause a person to want to continue those acts. But, people also find it upsetting to see someone else being credited, applauded, advanced, and so forth for another person's work or actions that are really not praiseworthy. Equally as upsetting is when a person's accomplishments and hard work are ignored or taken for granted. These types of behavior offend our sense of fairness. People are willing to share the limelight, but they also want to be recognized and to see others recognized for the role they played in an organization's success. It is also easier for people to accept constructive criticism from the leader for not accomplishing tasks if they know that praise will follow when they do. Praising productivity encourages people to be even more productive.

A Word of Caution

In order to be effective, praise must be for a legitimate accomplishment as opposed to a manufactured one. If every little contribution is accompanied by a response that greatly exceeds the achievement, its positive effect is lost. Recognition must fit the deed, and there must always be a fair balance between accomplishment and reward.

Suppose a member arranges all the details of an important dinner meeting and does an outstanding job. Publicly praising the member with perhaps a gift of dinner for two at a good restaurant would be appropriate, but honoring that member with a testimonial dinner would be excessive and lose its positive effect. Overkill has the reverse effect of what was intended. A spoonful of sugar makes the medicine go down, but a whole cup makes the child sick. Positive reinforcement and reasonable praise are essential motivators for members of an organization.

Chapter 2
The Leader's To-Do List

There are three requirements to becoming a good leader:

First: Possessing the right qualities (i.e., "The Right Stuff" as delineated in Chapter 1)

Second: Having the ability to apply those qualities in a way that inspires others to follow

Third: Being emotionally suited to assume a leadership position

Having "The Right Stuff" identifies leadership potential, but success is dependent upon its application. There is a difference between wanting good things to happen and making them happen. Those who want are followers; those who make are leaders.

Many people have the qualities needed to lead and the ability to apply those qualities, but different leadership roles provide different emotional needs. A person may be emotionally suited for one role but very inappropriate for another. Know thyself. Thus, when you have decided to pursue a specific leadership position, the answers to the following questions (in relationship to that position) will help you determine whether or not that specific role is the correct choice for you.

- ✓ Do you have the necessary coping skills to deal with the many pressures this specific role will bring to you from both the personal and professional arenas of your life?
- ✓ Can you remain calm and objective in emotionally charged situations, especially when someone disagrees with you?
- ✓ Will you enjoy the challenges this leadership role provides and not personalize the many complex issues that you will face along the way?
- ✓ Can you be consistent and unemotional when you make leadership decisions in this role?
- ✓ Can you assimilate experiences into a system of learning (e.g., on-the-job training) that will help you to address new challenges as they emerge?

✓ Can you put real and theoretical knowledge together in a way that will work for you and the organization you lead?

The difference between having the knowledge and possessing the skill becomes apparent when those skills must be applied to resolving practical matters. For instance, a pilot may possess all the necessary skills to navigate an airborne plane, but, if he cannot accomplish the takeoff, his services have no value to the airline. However, with proper training, the pilot will be able to correct those technical deficiencies and successfully complete flight assignments. Knowing what to do and how to do it are two entirely different things.

The world is full of might have beens. We grieve missed opportunities. A piece of Walter Mitty is in all of us. We fall into the "only if" cycle and grieve for the lost opportunities of yesterday while neglecting the opportunities of today. For the frustrated leader, those unfulfilled dreams are the result of personality flaws, limited ability, and/or poor training One may have the natural ability to be a leader, but, without some help, either formal (training) or informal (experience), that potential will never be actualized. There are many diamonds that never emerge from the rough! Leadership is an acquired skill whose mentors are training and experience.

1. Knowing Thyself

As an aphrodisiac, power ranks at the top of the list. All too often the quest for leadership causes individuals to confuse the person they want to be with the person they really are. You must be introspective. You must take a hard look at yourself and make a determination as to whether or not the leadership role you seek is a position you can successfully fulfill. Are you seeking the position for the right reasons? Are you competent to occupy the position you are pursuing?

The Peter Principle is a theory of leadership advanced in the late-1960s by Dr. Laurence Johnston Peter. Briefly stated, it identifies a leader's ability to perform in respective leadership roles as being one step below the competency level required to successfully do the job. "People rise to their level of incompetence," Peter said. Cynical? Yes! True? Often! Introspective people have a better sense of their level of competency.

When not blinded by ambition, people usually know what they are capable of doing or not doing. The poet Robert Browning wrote, "A man's reach should exceed his grasp or what's a heaven for." This makes great poetry, but, in reality, it may well be a blueprint for disaster. When seeking a leadership position, grasping beyond one's reach can become a prescription for personal and organizational destruction. Browning's heaven may well become another person's hell. Socrates believed the nonexamined life is not worth living and people must know what their capabilities and limitations are if they are to live successfully and harmoniously. Allowing one's self to be blinded by the lure of power can have a devastating effect upon not only the person involved but also everyone in that person's environment.

Five years ago, in an unnamed corporation, a person was temporarily promoted to a position to fill a vacancy at a level above him. The vacancy was unanticipated and required a physical presence with authority to maintain the status quo. The understanding was that the assignment would be short-term and the compensation would be substantial for the time the person served in the new assignment. The corporate plan was to fill the vacancy as soon as possible with a permanent replacement.

The corporate leaders initially planned to seek a replacement from outside the existing organization. Many successful managerial tools were already in place. The resigning employee was extremely successful and had planned for the smooth transition to a competent successor. Because of this, the interim appointee experienced almost immediate success.

Although he knew he was not suited for the position, the interim began to believe his short-term successes were actually the result of his efforts as opposed to his predecessor's hard work. He began to believe he had abilities he never had before. His thoughts were similar to that of the little boy who was invited to sit in the airplane captain's chair. The child began to believe he was flying the plane because he was allowed to hold the flight stick. Like the little boy, because the interim was allowed to fill the seat, he believed that he was actually doing the job. So, he lobbied for and received the permanent assignment.

Unfortunately, as time passed and new situations developed, his performance was less than satisfactory. But, he had become accustomed to the additional salary and the prestige of the new assignment. He could not go back, and he could not succeed. He floundered. His prior good reputation was quickly forgotten. The corporation terminated him.

The end of this sad story is that the man left his profession in disgrace to seek employment in a more favorable environment that was better suited to his capabilities. The tragedy was that he should have known that it was the wrong job for him. But, he did not know of his weakness for money or power. He was blinded by ambition. He suffered, his family suffered, and the people he was employed to serve suffered. He did not know himself; thus, he self-destructed.

Good leaders perform within the parameters that their abilities define for them.

You must find personal satisfaction in what you choose to do. True, there are good days and bad days in every leadership position. But, if the bad days outnumber the good, it usually means the decision to assume that leadership position was a bad one. Ambition can sometimes cloud judgment about what is good and what is bad. Good leaders know themselves! A decision to accept a leadership position must be a selfish decision, but accepting it for the wrong reasons can result in unhappiness and personal disaster. Know thyself!

2. Identify Your Leadership Philosophy

Leaders bring preconceived notions to their position of leadership that influence the actions they take and decisions they make. These preconceptions become loosely packaged into what eventfully becomes a leadership philosophy. Part of being a successful leader is to know your philosophy and how to apply it. Thus, as part of the process of knowing thyself, consider the following questions. Your answers will help you to identify what your present leadership leanings are and what you want them to be.

Do you agree or disagree with the following statements? (Check one)

	Agree	Disagree
A. Leaders are born, not made.	_____	_____
B. People are self-motivated and self-directed.	_____	_____
C. Work is God's gift to mankind.	_____	_____
D. Spare the rod, spoil the child.	_____	_____
E. A camel is a horse designed by a committee.	_____	_____
F. Security is the most important concern people have.	_____	_____
G. The average person likes/accepts responsibility.	_____	_____
H. A worker can be trusted to perform as expected.	_____	_____
I. Management is responsible to look after workers.	_____	_____
J. The average person prefers to be directed.	_____	_____

After you have completed this brief questionnaire, set it aside until you have reached page 37-38. There, you will find an analysis of your answers that will help you to identify your philosophical leanings.

Constancy, Predictability, Dependability

To be a successful leader, you must have an overall philosophy of leadership that is consistently applied to every leadership situation. Being consistent makes you predictable; being predictable enables people to know what they can and cannot expect of you. It is this consistency that is an invaluable tool in leading members towards meeting the organizational goals. Consistency and predictability help members understand leadership expectations and the intensity by which you will pursue established goals. It also forecasts how you will address negative and positive happenings that influence the successful completion of a designated task.

Your managerial philosophy evolves from your professional and personal experiences, coupled with the magnitude of your humanism—or lack thereof. How you behave towards people is reflective of those interpersonal experiences that become an intricate part of your personality. If you follow a particular philosophy of management, decisions made and actions taken can be applied to the practical application of that philosophy. If an action you take or a decision you make meets your philosophical criteria, then you are functioning consistently. However, if it does not, then you are acting inconsistently and must make certain behavioral changes to bring your actions into line with your philosophy. If this is not done, then the membership will become confused and unsure of what your expectations are.

Predictability and dependability are very important aspects of successful leadership. Predictability has already been discussed; dependability is an extension of the term. The leader whose behavior is predictable under a specific set of circumstances can be depended upon to act in the manner that has been predicted. It is the combination of being predictable and dependable that enables a leader to be consistent.

For instance, suppose you expect members of your organization to arrive at meetings prepared and on time. Past behavior has shown that, when a member is unprepared or is tardy without a legitimate reason for being so, you react negatively. (It does not matter what the reaction is for the purpose of this explanation.) Either consciously or subconsciously, the members depend upon you for this reaction. If you do not react as anticipated, they become confused because you are no longer predictable. Subsequent situations become confusing or chaotic to a membership that is attempting to follow you.

Many examples of management philosophies emerged in the mid-1950s. Douglas McGregor, who in the early 1950s was professor of management at the prestigious Alfred P. Sloan School of Management at MIT, articulated the most definitive theory. McGregor wrote what became the most authoritative management bible of the time, *The Human Side of Enterprise*, which categorized various leadership styles and made them more popularly recognized as Theory X and

Theory Y. He theorized that management styles evolve from one of two opposing views regarding human behavior.

Theory X

According to McGregor, the underlining belief of a Theory X manager is that:

- ✓ The average human being has an inherent dislike for work and will avoid it if he can.
- ✓ Because of this human characteristic of dislike of work, most people must be coerced, controlled, directed, and threatened with punishment to get them to put forth adequate effort toward the achievement of organizational objectives.
- ✓ The average human being prefers to be directed, wishes to avoid responsibility, has relatively little ambition, and wants security above all.

Based upon these beliefs, a leader who is not confident of the work ethic of his followers manages in a particular way. In most cases, the management style is that of a strict taskmaster who applies dogmatic systems of accountability.

Theory Y

McGregor believed that a Theory Y manager was the converse of Theory X. A Theory Y manager believes that:

- ✓ The expenditure of physical and mental effort in work is as natural as play or rest.
- ✓ External controls and threats of punishment are not the only means for bringing about effort towards organizational objectives. Man will exercise self-direction and self-control in the service of objectives to which he is committed.
- ✓ Commitment to objectives is a function of the rewards associated with their achievement.
- ✓ The average human being learns, under proper conditions, not only to accept but to seek responsibility.
- ✓ The capacity to exercise a relatively high degree of imagination, ingenuity, and creation in the solution of organizational problems is widely, not narrowly distributed in the population.
- ✓ The intellectualities of the average human being are only partially utilized under the conditions of modern industrial life.

Theory Z

A third theory of management, Theory Z, was developed later in the mid-1980s by William Ouchi. Ouchi analyzed the Japanese style of supervision and management. According to Ouchi, a Theory Z manager believes that:

- ✓ Workers are self-actualized and want to be a part of something of meaning and substance.
- ✓ A worker must be loyal to the organization.
- ✓ Workers have a great thirst for knowledge about their organization and want to play a major part in its development.
- ✓ The worker can be trusted to perform as management expects them to perform.
- ✓ A worker should progress up through the ranks, learning all aspects of the operation. This builds loyalty to the organization and its goals.
- ✓ Management has a responsibility to look after their workers.
- ✓ Workers want to share in the decision-making process to advance the goals of the organization.
- ✓ A work environment must support family, culture, and tradition with equal vigor as it supports productivity.

Practically speaking of course, a leader's style is not completely Theory X or Theory Y or Theory Z. However, a greater tendency is always toward one management style over the others.

Your management style is dependent upon your personality. Your approach to various life situations has been developed over a long period of time because of many positive and negative experiences. You will naturally articulate one style more than the others because it is part of your persona. A management style is based upon your inner belief about the attitudes and capabilities of mankind; this belief is articulated in your actions and in the kinesthetic messages that you send. Uncontrolled reflexive messages transmit your true feelings, despite words or actions to the contrary. If you want to change your style of management, you must first change the underlining beliefs that cause you to think and behave in a particular way. Otherwise, your body will send one message while your actions will send another. This lack of consistency will greatly impede the accomplishment of the established goals of the organization. Inconsistency and confusion are major impediments to successful leadership.

It is not my intention to advocate one management style of leadership over another. Your preference as both a member and leader may differ significantly from another. Indeed, history is replete with numerous examples of exceptional leaders in all categories. You may not agree with a particular philosophy or where a leader may choose to lead followers. But, because you may disagree with the goals of a particular enterprise, it does not necessarily negate the accomplishments—either positive or negative—of that leader. After a thousand years, historians cannot agree on an evaluation of Julius Caesar as a man. But, the fact that he was an effective leader is beyond challenge. How about George Patton? Douglas MacArthur? Woodrow Wilson? The names of leaders representing Theory X, Y, or Z leadership styles could fill volumes. The facts are that, if the membership and the mission are compatible and if the leader possesses the qualities of a good leader for that mission and for those members, that leader will be successful, regardless of the merits of the mission or the chosen style of management.

Your primary focus must be on the mission. Clearly, there are preferred ways to approach a given situation; however, to achieve a goal, you may choose to use a variety of styles. Thus, you can shift from "Let's plan it together" (Theory Z) to "I trust you to do the job" (Theory Y) to "Do it or else" (Theory X). The issue is the doughnut, not the hole. The style you employ to meet goals is less important than actually meeting the goal.

The primary ingredient for successful leadership is compatibility between you and your members.

What members expect from their leader is threefold:

First: To set a course of action for all to follow, they expect the leader to provide a direction.

Second: To do the very best job that he or she is capable of doing, effort counts.

Third: To hold members accountable, they must fulfill the responsibilities of their assignment.

When poor performance is ignored by you or not addressed in a meaningful way, it undermines the initiative of the entire organization. Members expect you to hold member's feet to the fire. When this does not happen, morale, respect, and enthusiasm erode at a rapid rate.

Your Leadership Philosophy

In terms of your philosophical leanings as they relate to your answers to the leadership questionnaire on page 33, consider the following:

If you agreed with statement letters A, D, E, F, and J, you have tendencies towards Theory X. The more questions you agreed with, the stronger you are feeling.

If you agreed with statement letters B, C, G, H, and I, you have tendencies towards Theory Y or Z. The more questions you agreed with, the stronger you are feeling.

> Theory Y and Z are packaged together because they represent the humanistic approach to leadership and are very similar in their practice and belief. On the other hand, Theory X represents an opposing philosophy.

If you are satisfied with your philosophical position and believe it best represents your leadership beliefs, then being consistent is simply a matter of measuring each decision you make against your convictions. If each decision is consistent, you are well on your way to being predictable, and dependable. If not, then it is time to reevaluate your philosophy and the decisions you make to bring both into conformity.

3. Learn About the Organization

Successful leaders must be knowledgeable of all aspects of the organization they lead. Above all, they must understand its mission as well as the principles upon which it was founded. As a leader, you should obtain the answers to the following questions:

General Questions

- ✓ Why was the organization formed?
- ✓ What is its mission?
- ✓ Does the organization have a constitution and bylaws?
- ✓ What is the financial status of the organization?
- ✓ What are the past successes of the organization?
- ✓ What are the past failures of the organization?
- ✓ Why were they considered to be failures?

Organizational Questions

- ✓ Does the organization have an overriding governing body?
- ✓ What is the process by which decisions are made and executed?
- ✓ Does the organization have goals and a plan to meet those goals?
- ✓ How are funds raised and expended?
- ✓ How is one appointed or removed from a committee?

Structural Questions

- ✓ What are the organizational qualifications for membership?
- ✓ What are the organizational qualifications for leaders?
- ✓ Does the organization have officers with defined responsibilities?
- ✓ How do officers (or other organizational leaders) become officers?

The more you learn about the organization, the greater the probability is for success. An organization's history is important for future organizational development. Not knowing about an organization's history may cause your organization to ineffectively and inefficiently utilize time and resources because past errors can easily be repeated. An organization that fails to learn from the past is destined to repeat it. In many organizations, visionary leaders have kept a record in booklet or pamphlet format of the organization's history so that new members have the information at their fingertips. Organizations that have not developed an historical transcript should consider doing so. This practice has become common as groups realize their history is a source of pride and inspiration. It connects the past to the future in a way that reaffirms the principles upon which an organization was founded.

Your responsibility is to be true to the organization's mission, meet its goals, and articulate the desires of its membership. You may influence or change the thinking of the membership, but you must reflect its present thinking during the transitional stage. When pursuing a leadership position, you must learn the organization's expectations for its leader in order to determine whether or not it will be a good fit for you and for them. If there is not a high level of compatibility, then the organization must select a different leader—one who is better suited to serve the needs of that organization.

All organizations have rules and operational procedures. Sometimes, they are written down; sometimes, they are based upon tradition or past practice. But, in all cases (other than dire emergencies), the old way of conducting business must be respected until they are changed through established channels. This process may take longer, but it is the correct way and will be better understood by the membership. This kind of discipline brings about orderly change. Orderly change avoids confusion and disorder. It enables organizational goals to be developed and achieved while evolving to a new type of leadership.

Leaders who place themselves above the rules create a free-for-all management system in which everyone does their own thing. When this occurs, nothing positive can happen. Change must take place systematically within the framework of the existing structure. If this is not within your personality to do so, your organization will have a difficult time establishing and meeting goals.

Guidelines

Guidelines define the operational parameters of the organization you lead. If you disagree with these guidelines, you must work from within the existing framework to change them. If you choose not to operate within existing guidelines, the membership will also ignore those very same guidelines. The end result will be a breakdown of order and discipline throughout the organization. Here is a case in which leading by example plays a critical role in setting the proper tone. It is a matter of structure and discipline. Cute expressions like "Rules are made to be broken" do not work in this situation.

An Organizational Marriage

At one time, Benito Mussolini provided excellent leadership to the Italian people. He was a Fascist in a country that required a fascist leader. For several years, that marriage was a successful one. His leadership style and political philosophy matched his country's need. Had he embraced a communist philosophy or a democratic philosophy, he would have failed. It was a matter of pairing. Franklin Delano Roosevelt met the needs of the American people, and Joseph Stalin regrettably met the needs of the Russian people. Any juxtaposition of people, circumstances, or geographic locations would have resulted in failure for those leaders. (This is exactly what happened to Mussolini when circumstances changed.) These leaders were the right people for a period of time in the historical evolution of their respective countries.

Your ability to lead is only part of the equation. It must be the right marriage, or you will fail. A good leader or even a great leader may be good for one organization, but devastating for another. The sage advice of "Look before you leap" could not be more appropriate then when you are seeking a leadership position.

4. Understand the Responsibilities and Limitations of the Office

Having a clear understanding of the organization's mission is critical to a leader's ability to successfully lead. Without that understanding, the organization will lack a purpose and a direction. Thus, as a prerequisite to good leadership, you must obtain the answers to the following questions:

- ✓ What are the organization's mission and goals?
- ✓ What do members of an organization expect of their leader?
- ✓ What is the leader's authority?
- ✓ What are the limitations?

✓ What resources are available to assist in completing the mission?

As the leader, you must rely upon two factors to successfully accomplish an organizational goal. The first relates to your ability and determination. You must be competent. The second relates to external sources that may or may not be under your control. These resources are not dependent upon your competency; they are resources such as money, staffing, equipment, and so forth. But, if these resources are not available or if they are available but not placed under your control, your ability to meet organizational goals will be seriously impeded. Under these circumstances, unless there is something unique about this particular leadership position, I would discourage you from accepting it.

Another area of responsibility is the matter of loyalty. Leaders have a primary responsibility to be loyal to those they represent. At times, meeting this responsibility can become very difficult when attempting to resolve organizational conflicts, especially those that involve both members and nonmembers. In a work-related environment in which the leader has a responsibility to the employer as well as to the member, there will be times when leaders must face issues of conflicting loyalties. These situations become more complicated when a leader has been elected to represent labor and there is a labor/management conflict. If the leader's role is to represent labor, there is no question as to where the leader's support should be. The leader must be the voice of labor.

Suppose the relationship is supervisor/subordinate? Does that leader owe the membership blind support as part of the leadership role? What if the member is wrong and the institution is correct? These are difficult issues to resolve and unfortunately are all too common, especially in small companies in which everyone is somehow connected to one another. However, there are overriding moral issues that must serve as a beacon in the darkness and confusion of the decision-making process. The leader must always be mindful of The Leadership Trinity—credibility, honesty, and integrity (as defined in Chapter 1).

The solution to these problems is twofold:

First: You must never be disloyal to the member.
Second: You must always do the morally correct thing.

If the member is wrong, you have a responsibility to be honest and forthright with the member behind closed doors. However, on the other side of the door, you must support the member while attempting to convince him or her to alter the existing course of action.

The membership is not entitled to your blind support. Your responsibility is to provide the recalcitrant member with every service to which membership entitles him or her. But, you do not have a responsibility to publicly embrace a wrongful act or pursue a dishonest course of action. Part of having The Right Stuff is a leader's commitment to credibility, honesty, and integrity. This is the mantra of a good leader. The honorable way is not usually the easier way, but it is the right way. My father used to say, "No hat, regardless of its size, is big enough for two heads." Now I understand why.

If the membership expects you to give up the right to make fair and objective determinations on related organizational issues, then this expectation must be clearly understood before you seek a leadership position. A leader of integrity would not accept it. How many doctors are leaving the employment of HMOs because they cannot accept their policies for administrating appropriate medical care? How many stay just because it is their job? Expressions such as "It's lonely at the top" are generated by factual experiences. In most organizations, it is difficult to be a leader because of the clashes between one's personal morality, one's conception of right and wrong, and the responsibilities one has to the institution and to the individuals involved.

Suppose a person in an organization or department is pressing forward on a course of action that is in opposition to the directive of that member's immediate supervisor? To further complicate matters, suppose the member is correct and the institution is wrong? Beyond making available to the member all his or her entitled rights and benefits, what else is the leader expected to do?

The leader's job is to make sure that organizational commitments to the member are kept. Beyond that, the leader's course of action must be dictated by analyzing the existing circumstances and making the morally correct decision without being disloyal to the member or the organization. The kiss of death for a leader is delivered at the exact moment the leader violates the personal trust of the membership. In fact, even the perception that a leader has questionable loyalty makes it extremely difficult for that person to lead and for members to follow.

Solutions to conflicting situations are not easy to find, but they can be solved. You must have a keen sense of right and wrong and the courage to embrace a morally correct position. A good leader really does not have a choice. This is a matter of personal and professional integrity. Even when you disagree with a member's actions, you must make available whatever services and protections that are provided as part of membership.

Every effort must be made to counsel a member who is in the wrong to do the right thing. Of course, the member has a free will and must suffer the consequences of a bad decision. As long as you have been honest with the member and have provided entitled services as needed, there is nothing more that can be done. Sometimes people just have to self-destruct. This is how some learn right from wrong and when to hold and when to fold. There are people in all walks of life that must learn the hard way. But, this is all part of leadership. What first begins as an issue of loyalty can easily become one of credibility, honesty, and integrity.

5. Read the Tea Leaves

You must be hyper vigilant! You must be current on all activities of the organization as well as any social and political situations that may impact membership. Your role is analogous to that of a sea captain who is forever observing and looking for changes in tides, shorelines, and water currents. You must know as much about your world as the sea captain knows about his world. The mission of the captain is to bring the ship to a safe harbor. You must also bring your organization to a safe harbor in your respective role as organizational caretaker.

Specifically, you must be aware of:

✓ Your own emotional state
✓ The emotional state of others
✓ Environmental and social changes that impact organizational goals

Emotional State of the Leader

You must be in control of your emotions at all times. You must be aware of and cautious of mood swings that influence your behavior and decision making. For instance, if you are having a bad day, you must be careful not to direct misplaced anger toward the wrong person. Similarly, a rush of euphoria can cause you to be overly generous.

Haven't we all delayed a question to a parent, boss, spouse, or friend until they were in a good mood because we wanted a particular decision to be made a particular way? The organization's members observe our moods and behavior for the same reasons. They wait until the most favorable time to approach us in the hope that our mood will work in their favor. Good leaders must maintain composure and objectivity because we make sounder decisions when our emotions are under control. Objectivity is a major element of good leadership.

Emotional State of Others

You must be aware of the emotional state of others. Taking a harsh but justified action toward a recalcitrant member who recently experienced a death of a loved one is never excused by saying, "I didn't know." This is not an acceptable excuse because leaders are expected to know, and knowing requires you to be approachable, available, and concerned. You must be observant. Sensitive people notice emotional changes in other people and adjust their own behavior accordingly.

This awareness enables you to offer encouragement when needed, calm apprehensions when appropriate, offer personal counseling when requested, and to make an objective assessment of the course of action to follow as situations evolve. Sensitivity reassures people of their worth to the organization and of your concern for their well-being.

Social and Environmental Changes

You must be the eyes of your organization and be aware of any social or environmental changes that influence it. Neither you nor your organization can operate in a vacuum. We live in a world of interdependencies that, at times, seem to be unrelated but actually have a great deal in common with one another. If something is happening that is going to impact the organization, you must have a system in place (such as the ICN suggested in Chapter 1) to kept you current and responsive. You must anticipate the future and act upon it.

For instance, suppose a charitable organization decides to hold a fund-raising function at a specific location and time. The function's success will depend upon community attendance and support. If your organization is not aware of the fund-raising calendar of other groups when planning your own fund-raising activity, there is a significant risk of having conflicting schedules that will hinder both organizations' efforts to raise needed capital. Similarly, national organizations holding annual conventions need to know the annual convention schedule of other organizations if they want to maximize membership attendance. Organizations and their leaders must be aware of each other's existence, mission, and future plans. People, organizations, and their respective activities are the tea leaves; together, they tell the future. You must learn to read them.

6. Have a Plan

> *"A goal without a plan is just a dream that has little chance of coming true."*
> —Linda Thomas, Social Worker

An organization must have a mission, and, to complete it, an organization must follow a road map, that is, The Plan. But crafting The Plan is only the beginning of the process. Without established procedures, the delegation of tasks, monitoring, record keeping, follow-up, and assessment, a Plan is nothing more than an unfulfilled wish list. Attention to details turns The Plan into reality. The Plan gives an organization its direction—defining where it is going and how it will get there.

The Planning Check List

Providing detailed instruction on how to develop a comprehensive organizational Plan exceeds the scope and intent of this book. Bookstores, libraries, and the Internet have an endless supply of resource material intended for this very purpose. Obviously, a Plan must be designed to accommodate the needs of the organization being served, and the planning must be done by those in the organization who have the authority and capability to do so. A good plan always begins with shared decision making. This being said, there is a commonality among good plans. The checklist below reflects some of that commonality. However, different organizations require plans that reflect the purpose and the mission of that organization and may not fit the mold that is being presented. This is a case where one size does not fit all.

✓ A Plan's desired outcome must be within the parameters of the organization's mission statement, that is, its purpose in being.

✓ A Plan begins by defining what it is intended to accomplish.

✓ A Plan must include a realistic timeline for completion.

✓ A Plan must provide for evaluative checkpoints along the way.

✓ A Plan must define the resources needed and available to successfully complete it.

✓ A Plan must be adjustable as circumstances dictate.

✓ A Plan must include an evaluation component for use upon completion which measures its value to the organization as well as its success or failure.

Throughout this section, some checklist items have been addressed in greater detail than others. However, Plans differ with the type and intent of the organization, and designers must know both before planning can begin.

The Three R's—Revisit, Reevaluate, Redesign

Once your Plan has been developed and realistic timelines have been established, a cyclical program of continual evaluations must be implemented that enables the organization to rethink its various aspects and to make adjustments as necessity dictates. Every plan must be revisited often, reevaluated against the organizational mission, and redesigned as needed. The Plan should never become so entrenched that it becomes carved in stone. It is the mission that determines The Plan, not The Plan that determines the mission.

A Plan defines an organization's path. Each and every part of it should be geared towards fulfilling specific goals. Thus, every goal, every modification, and every quest must be measured in terms of the organization's mission. If any part of it does not fit, it should be deleted. Plans must be achievable, adjustable, amendable, or disposable. Although a Plan may define the organization during a particular period of time, it never becomes more important than the survival of the organization itself. If the mission or the goals of the organization change, the Plan must be amended to reflect the newly defined mission or related goals.

When travelers ask the American Automobile Association (AAA) to plan a driving route to a specific destination, AAA provides a detailed map called a Trip Tik. This is a very specific blueprint (road map) that provides the most efficient route to the final destination. However, circumstances may develop that require the traveler to vary from that plan. When they do, the AAA simply develops another one. In other words, the Trip Tik steers them to a point until it becomes necessary to modify it. It would be foolish for travelers to say, "No, we must follow the original map" when they have changed their immediate or long-term destination.

Organizations should function the same way. They have their Trip Tik (Plan), and, like the traveler, they will revise their Plan (road map) when they have a reason to do so, but the entire map is rarely discarded. Relevant points are kept; others are not. At all times, the mission defines the destination.

Constructing the Organization Trip Tik

Organizational stakeholders must play a part in developing The Plan. This inclusion is vital to the shared decision-making process. Involving others does not guarantee a plan's success, but not involving others generally guarantees its failure. It is a universally understood that "The man who rows the boat generally doesn't have time to rock it." The plan must be comprehensive and must address the short- and long-term goals of the organization. The more detailed each component of The Plan is, the better the organizational Trip Tik. The mission dictates what must be done (the what); the Plan defines the matters of how, when, and where certain aspects must be implemented.

When your organization finalizes its overall Plan, the lead person for each goal must develop a sub-Plan using a similar format to address the same items in greater detail. For instance, if part of the plan is to raise money for a particular project, a subcommittee might decide to have an auction and then plan the specifics such as time, location, and so forth. Comprehensive planning at all levels with plenty of lead time will substantially increase the possibilities for success. When there is sufficient time to plan, there is less pressure, fewer mistakes, and more objective decision making.

When your plan is completed, goals must be prioritized. When establishing priorities, issues such as "most important—less important" must be decided. Establishing priorities does not fall into place on its own. Sometimes, establishing priorities requires as much time as it takes to develop the actual plan. Even so, when established, a progression that goes from most important to least important may not be the correct or most feasible path to follow. For instance, the most important goal may be one that is not affordable within the established timeline. Or perhaps, a key person needed to lead a subcommittee will not be available for an extended period of time. However, several less significant goals might be achieved that would be helpful in advancing an organization's agenda. These are just a few of the variables that might impact the completion of a priority in the desired order or timeline. You must consider all variables when priorities are established. But, once again, the earlier the planning sessions are held in the time continuum, the better it will be for the entire organization.

Implementing the Plan

When your planning has been completed and the priorities have been established, the next step is Implementation. At this stage, the key word is monitoring. Does this goal make sense? Is it progressing according to plan? Does it need to be revised or reevaluated? Is the project meeting the timeline? Should it be revised? Necessity, of course, will determine when the Plan should be revisited. Certainly, at least one meeting a year should be devoted to this purpose. The key is that every plan be subject to review and modified as circumstances dictate. People change, priorities shift, and other needs develop. Flexibility is an absolute necessity.

Longevity

One final word about planning: the organization's goals and its comprehensive plan should exceed the leader's term of office. Successors should have a direction to follow or amend accordingly. The organization's advancement is a continuous process whose lifetime should not be limited by the longevity of the leadership. If planning and transition are done correctly, new leaders can work within the established framework to make the changes to the organizational plans they deem appropriate. A leader has a responsibility not only to respect the past but also to protect the future. The goal should be to have seamless changes in leadership. It is your responsibility and an organization's legacy to have a plan for the future.

7. Learn How to Run a Meeting

Few people would place attendance at meetings as something that ranks high on their list of "things I enjoy doing," but, until the time when the human race becomes telepathic, meetings will continue to be a necessary evil.

A large percentage of the business conducted by organizations takes place in meetings. Some meetings are small in size and designed to perform limited tasks. Others are on a larger scale and may involve a significant part of, if not the entire, membership. Even in this age of faxes, e-mails, and computers, meetings are still an efficient and effective way to communicate with the membership.

However, meetings poorly planned and conducted are deadly. Despite the fact they provide an opportunity for leadership to accomplish a broad range of organizational tasks in a short period of time, many leaders miss their opportunities because they lack the necessary skills to conduct a good meeting. The result of poorly planned and executed meetings is that attendees consider them to be a waste of time. If attendance is voluntary, it declines rapidly, and the organization must find alternative, less efficient ways of conducting business.

When meetings are poorly planned and/or executed, opportunities are lost, and the entire organization suffers. A leader who lacks the ability to effectively run a meeting should make a personal commitment to acquire those needed skills. A good place to start is to review how specific meetings of the past were conducted by previous leaders or chairpersons. Two lists should be developed: one should record aspects of the meetings that were good (e.g., chairperson started on time and so forth) and the other should list aspects that were bad (e.g., poorly constructed agenda and so forth). In all future meetings when the leader serves as chairperson, the listed bad aspects must be conscientiously avoided. Likewise, the listed good aspects should be emulated at every opportunity. In addition, the following suggestions will work wonders for anyone who wishes to learn:

✓ There must be a valid reason for holding a meeting. Meetings without a purpose waste time and reflect poorly on the entire leadership team; they should never be called. Not only must a meeting have a purpose; that purpose should be made known to all prospective attendees.

✓ Meetings should be held in locations that are appropriate to housing them. Beginning with holding the meeting in an area of sufficient size to accommodate all attendees, there should be appropriate seating with visibility for all attendees to see each speaker and view the required visual aides.

✓ Depending upon the length and intent of the meeting, serving light refreshments addresses a social need of attendees and assists in making attending a meeting a more pleasant experience. In most cases, it helps to set an appropriate tone.

✓ Meeting rooms should be acoustically prepared so that all speakers and media presentations can be heard by all attendees.

✓ Meeting rooms should be protected from unnecessary interruptions.

✓ An agenda should be prepared and made available with sufficient time for revision and distribution before the date of the scheduled meeting. Additional copies should be available at the time of the meeting. This agenda should be comprehensive in identifying location, date, time, plus all items to be discussed. This agenda may be constructed by the leader, a committee, or both. Regardless of how it is constructed, it should provide for input from the membership. When the agenda is accepted and circulated, it should be followed. Variations should be rare and for a good reason. If the agenda is properly planned, the need for variations will be minimal.

✓ Agenda items should be varied; breaking up topics help to keep people focused.

✓ If material is to be circulated as part of the meeting, there should be a sufficient number of handouts so that attendees who require them should have their own copies. If attendees do not have to share their agenda, they are better able to give the chairperson their undivided attention.

✓ There should be a meeting format that is consistently followed at each organizational meeting. Variation from that format should happen only under the most unusual of circumstances. This consistency will help attendees know what to expect with subsequent meetings.

✓ Meetings should start on time, and established timelines should be strictly adhered to from beginning to its end. This requirement places a greater responsibility on the agenda planner(s) to think the meeting out and to anticipate all the variables before the agenda is finalized.

✓ Once the meeting has been called to order, all sidebar meetings and conversations should stop immediately. If the meeting is important, the chairperson should have the attendees' undivided attention. If the meeting is not important, it should not have been called in the first place. Attendees who feel that they need to continue with side conversations should be asked to remove themselves to an area where they can continue unimpeded. Chitchat is acceptable before and after a meeting—never during.

✓ Discussions on agenda items should be kept on track with limited variations. The stricter the adherence to an agenda topic, the more productive the meeting will be. Side issues, although agenda-related, should be avoided. The chairperson must keep the attendees on task.

✓ Some form of established or modified parliamentary procedures should be followed consistently in every meeting. All commentators and speakers should receive recognition from the chairperson before addressing the assembly. This is a primary responsibility of the chairperson. Other than issues relating to established rules of order, speakers not recognized by the chairperson are out of order and should be silenced by the chairperson.

✓ All people of standing on an agenda item should be allowed to address the assembly. However, the chairperson must closely monitor this to ensure the topic is addressed, repetition is kept to a minimum, and the agenda moves along. If in the process peripheral but non-relevant matters surface, they should be addressed at a different time. Each agenda item must be disposed of by resolution, action, deletion, or postponement. Agenda items cannot be ignored. If every person who has the right to speak knows they will have an opportunity to do so, order will prevail, and the meeting will follow the established sequence. However, it is the duty of the chairperson to control the meeting and all participants. This means that the chairperson cannot be a commentator or dominate the conversation. The chairperson must exercise self-control.

✓ As a general rule, short meetings are better than long ones. A short meeting is anything less than forty-five minutes. If a long meeting is necessary, refreshments should be provided, and appropriate break times should be incorporated. For the longer meeting, the recommendation that agenda items be varied must be implemented to maintain attendee interest.

✓ When a question is asked of the chairperson or another attendee, the chairperson should repeat the question before it is answered.
There are three reasons for this very important process:

First: Repeating the question keeps everyone focused because everyone knows what is going on.

Second: Repeating the question ensures its accuracy.

Third: Repeating the question ensures that everyone has heard it.

✓ When, in larger audiences, a question is asked of the chairperson or another attendee and is answered immediately without being repeated, it tends to set up a one-to-one conversation between the speakers to the exclusion of the audience. Repeating the question helps to avoid this problem. But, the chairperson must exercise common sense. There are times, especially in a small meeting, when it is not necessary. However, when in doubt, the chairperson should err on the side of repetition.

✓ The end time of a meeting should be known beforehand and closely followed. Over the long run, keeping to established timelines will ensure good and attentive attendance. It shows respect for the attendee's time. It also allows participants to plan their day with the remaining available time.

✓ Prior to adjournment, a designated party (usually the chairperson or secretary) should summarize key points of the meeting. The dates, times, and locations of future meetings should be established.

As a final note, a leader who understands the meeting process is rarely surprised at a meeting. When an agenda is developed, all possible variations of that agenda item should be anticipated, and anticipated problems should be resolved beforehand. Business meetings should not be the place where wars are waged. A leader who is in tune with the membership should be able to resolve many problems in other more appropriate forums.

8. Be a Consensus Builder

Shared decision making is at the very center of consensus building; consensus building is at the heart of shared decision making. Each process must coexist because each is dependent upon the other to be successful. And, if both are not present, the attempt to collaborate in a meaningful way will fail.

Shared Decision Making

For the purposes of this exploration, shared decision making is defined as a process of assigning the authority to make an organizational decision(s) to a subgroup of organization members who have been empowered by their respective constituents to act on the membership's behalf. The intent of this process is to involve and utilize the resources of membership in a meaningful and productive way in deciding on issues of importance to the organization. Members of the subgroup resolve specific issues in a collegial as opposed to an authoritative manner. When utilized successfully, membership will have a greater interest in the outcome of an organizational initiative because it has shared in and, therefore, has ownership of the decision.

You must establish a climate of shared decision making in which decisions are faced in an objective, unemotional way and are decided in the best interest of the organization. This requires patience, objectivity, compromise, and the suppression of your personal biases as a subgroup (sometimes called a team) works to arrive at an acceptable decision. Shared decision making requires a respect for the intellect, interest, and commitment of participating members who play various roles in the organizational structure. It is based upon a belief that intelligent reasoning (as opposed to intimidation and threats) is a more reliable method of achieving a satisfactory end. It is the true spirit of the collaborative process.

Exercising the authority that is intrinsic to a leadership position should rarely be used and only under the most extenuating of circumstances when the outstanding issue is critical to the organization and all available time to reach consensus has been exhausted.

Because shared decision making is a group process, decisions are rarely made with the rapidity of those made by individuals. However, the benefits derived from empowering membership are so superior to that of the authoritarian process that it is worth expending the time and energy to let the group decide.

If a subcommittee becomes deadlocked on a particular issue and realizes they are unable to decide, they will gladly turn to you to make decisions. Unless that point is reached, you must trust the process and let it take its course.

Consensus

A consensus is a significant number more than a majority. Decisions by consensus neither need nor require unanimous support; still, it must be clearly evident that the organizational support for a particular position is overwhelming. Unanimous support on an issue(s) may not be possible to achieve, but consensus is always necessary. There are times when political or personal considerations may prevent a member from supporting attempts to have unanimity on a particular issue, despite that person's belief that the action being contemplated is the correct one. For instance, perhaps a decision (albeit a correct one) may cause personal hardship for a friend (e.g., eliminating a job, changing a vendor, and so forth) or upset a family member. A person may not support an action in the affirmative, but might not interfere with the correct decision being made. There are many situations when unanimous support is not achievable, but consensus is.

To be a good consensus builder, you must be able to convince members through reasoning that, on its own merits, one decision is better for the organization than another. Every person of standing (i.e., one who has a legitimate right to be involved) on an issue should be able to express his or her opinions without prejudice. Threats and intimidation do not have a place in the consensus building process. When they are used, shared decision making becomes part of the organization's past; reduced volunteerism, limited membership input, and decreased enthusiasm become part of its future.

There are times when efforts to build a consensus are thwarted by conflicts among members within an organization. As the leader, your responsibility is to ameliorate or arrange for someone else to ameliorate any problems that impede the process. Disagreements or out-and-out disputes between members can frequently be handled through the astute mediation efforts of a competent leader who is perceived to be concerned and objective.

However, there will be times when objectivity and good reason will not bring about consensus. This should not prevent a decision from being made on worthwhile and important issues. If this is the case, you must move forward with the support of the majority. If you fail to secure majority support to act, then alternatives to the proposed course of action must be considered. The leader must not move ahead on an issue that is clearly not supported by the membership. Failing to reconsider and forcing an action the membership opposes puts your credibility and integrity into question. The negative overflow from this type of aggressive behavior will be so destructive that it can destroy the organization.

9. Be Objective

"Don't confuse him with facts; his mind is made up."

The last thing that should be said about you is that you are not objective. If accurate, this is a serious leadership flaw that could be fatal to any effort to build a collaborative organization. Maintaining objectivity is critical—not only in deciding upon organizational goals and specific projects to meet those goals but also in regulating interpersonal relationships. In a truly collaborative leadership, the free exchange of ideas is at the very core of an organization's success, but it requires objectivity to allow this exchange to take place.

The Veto

When developing a Plan or Goal you must have influence and the power and authority to veto a group decision. But, when the leader's determination becomes the only acceptable decision, the organization is no longer a collaborative one. It is a dictatorship, and most dictatorships are short-lived. A leader who interferes with the decision-making process because of a belief that the organization is making a bad decision—but is unable to convince the membership to decide otherwise—must yield on that issue to the will of the membership. Stating an opinion is a leader's right and responsibility; imposing it on a membership is a leader's ruination.

Vetoing or interfering with the implementation of an organizational undertaking represents the very worst kind of leadership. Regardless of a leader's authority to do so, the veto should never be used against any action or decision unless the action being considered violates the law. If there is going to be collaboration and shared decision making within the organization, you must remain objective because this is a process that is based upon respect and support for team decisions. Vetoing an organizational initiative is the antithesis of what shared decision making is all about.

Objectivity in Organizational Assignments

Generally, assignments are given to individuals based upon that person's ability to advance organizational goals. You cannot allow personal feelings and/or hostilities to interfere with assignment determinations. You must set personal affections and individual dislikes aside for the collective good. You must strive to make the most productive and objective assignments of organizational responsibilities. When a plan has been developed, you must concentrate on accomplishing the specifics of that plan. This process involves working with and deploying people as necessity dictates.

Good leaders do not set up obstacles to working with another person, team, or organization because of unrelated peripheral issues. Obstacles interfering with communication, collaboration, and cooperation must be removed. When a leader's vision is blinded by personal matters, it is incumbent upon that leader to yield the decision to others who are competent and will be more objective in making a particular decision. President George Bush (Sr.) was not a big fan of President Jimmy Carter. In fact, they had major disagreements on many issues. But, when it came time to seek intermediaries in foreign affairs, Carter was on Bush's first-call list. Why? Because Bush believed that, when dealing with specific foreign affairs, Carter was the best person for the job. The former baseball Yankee manager Casey Stengel despised the great Joe DiMaggio, and DiMaggio rarely spoke to Mickey Mantle. But, when it became necessary, personal feelings went into the background as they worked collaboratively to successfully complete the Yankee mission of winning World Championships. Objectivity is the secret to successful collaboration and shared decision making.

10. Delegate

> *"No man is an island."*
>
> —Thomas Merton

Delegating responsibilities to members is the most effective way to successfully complete the goals of an organization. You cannot and are not expected to do everything without help. Other than in a very small organization with a limited purpose, responsibilities must be assigned to various members if an organization's mission is to be fulfilled. The ability to delegate is an acquired skill that can make or break leaders and their organizations. A leader who is unable to delegate will experience minimal success at best. In this situation, an organization would be better advised to select a leader with broader-based leadership skills.

"Rules of Engagement" to implement delegation

- ✓ A leader must know the strengths and weaknesses of the organization's members to determine who has the ability to accept responsibility and who does not. Therefore, the leader must give a great deal of thought and research to the delegation process.
- ✓ Based upon the leader's objective analysis of membership skills, the best person to complete a specific task must be the person selected. This assignment is a direct reflection on the leader's ability to make good decisions.

✓ The ultimate responsibility for the success or failure of an assignment will always be the leaders. This is something that cannot be delegated. Harry Truman was correct in stating that "the buck stops here" (at the leader's desk).

✓ A leader must delegate, empower, and support those entrusted with a specific assignment.

✓ A support system must accompany delegation. When a leader has empowered a member, the leader must ensure the member has the resources needed to successfully complete the assignment.

✓ If the assignment is worthwhile and the delegate selected is the wrong choice, then the delegate, not the assignment, must be changed.

✓ In terms of ownership, success belongs to the entire membership. Failure belongs to the leader.

✓ A leader's ability to effectively delegate is ultimately determined by the success or failure of the assignment. "The proof is in the pudding."

Advantages of Delegating

✓ Delegation helps to keep the membership invested and focused on the goals of the organization.

✓ Delegation provides a greater opportunity for an organization to meet its goals in an efficient and more productive manner.

✓ Delegation makes an organization less dependent upon the leader and more dependent upon an organizational team as the decision-making process is spread out across the membership.

✓ Delegation provides an opportunity for an astute leader to be surrounded by competent members who can work collaboratively to meet the goals of the organization.

✓ Delegation reinforces the concept of collaboration and shared decision making through actions as opposed to words.

✓ Delegation provides a training ground for future leaders to acquire experience in fulfilling leadership roles.

Warnings

✓ Delegation must be taken seriously. A cavalier approach to this process by the leader will be harmful to the organization. How and to whom a leader assigns responsibilities sends a message regarding the leader's assessment of the worth of a particular project and of particular members.

✓ Delegates are frequently selected for the wrong reasons (e.g., because it was that person's idea, to appease someone, or to quiet a recalcitrant member). For instance, suppose a baseball team player suggests to the team manager that it would be a good idea to bunt the runner on first base to second. The manager agrees and implements the decision. The bunt is on! But, unless the player who made the suggestion is the best person to carry it out, another will be selected to execute it. A competent manager rightfully delegates that responsibility to the best person to do the job. Any other decision would be negligent. Yet, this mistake is made by organizational leaders time and time again.

✓ Delegation is a process that lends itself to membership abuse. How often do members complain that, every time they make a suggestion, they get another job? If the goal of the leader is to discourage volunteerism and the free exchange of ideas, that is the way to do it.

✓ Sometimes, bad suggestions are implemented and responsibilities delegated simply to appease a member or to move a long standing item off the leader's desk.

✓ Some leaders consistently delegate to a chosen few, regardless of who is the best qualified to carry out an assignment. This limits the opportunity for others to become involved in a meaningful way. It also causes resentment and tension among the members.

✓ In most organizations, there are recalcitrant members who refuse to volunteer. Over an extended period of time, this can undermine organizational efforts and create moral problems. The leader must confront this problem by speaking directly with the members in question. Frequently, a simple reminder of their importance to the organization will be sufficient to reactivate their interest. Teaming up with more enthusiastic members or having peers discuss their lack of involvement with them will, at times, yield positive results. The primary goal is to determine why they are less involved and to address those concerns. However, if all efforts fail, membership termination or activity isolation is a viable option for the leader. Members should not be forced to volunteer or be given assignments they do not intend to fulfill. Likewise, they should not be allowed to reap the benefits that are the result of the labor of others.

✓ Micromanagement is the biggest pitfall to the delegation process. Delegating a task to a member and telling that member what to do and how to do it is two different things. The latter is referred to as micromanagement. Leaders who micromanage have little confidence in the ability of those to whom they assign responsibility. "If you want something done right, do it yourself" is the mantra of the consummate micromanager. Leaders who function this way better serve the organization by not delegating because their attitude is offensive and counterproductive. Micromanagers usually burn themselves out in short order and are rarely reelected or reappointed once this personality quirk becomes apparent to all.

An Eye towards Tomorrow

It is your responsibility to continually search for leadership potential and help train replacements. You will occupy a small place in the time continuum of an organization. This truism is healthy and inevitable. Your time comes, it passes, and another takes your place. This circle of life helps extend an organization's life beyond the leader's term of office. Through the process of delegation, the membership has an opportunity to assess the abilities of colleagues and to cultivate future leaders. It is good for the organization.

A leader who delegates and empowers provides an invaluable service to the individual delegated as well as the entire membership. Leaders who believe they are irreplaceable should heed the words of General Colin Powell, who forewarns that you should "Never let your ego get so close to your position that, when your position goes, your ego goes with it." No one is indispensable, and you must prepare for the time when you are replaced. Delegation is part of that preparation.

11. Temper Honesty with Discretion

The issue of honesty should be a simple matter to address, but it isn't. If there were ever an issue that cries out for common sense and discretion, this is it. Honesty is the best policy…or is it? We have been taught this "Golden Rule" from day one. After all, didn't George Washington confess to the cherry tree assault? How about Old Honest Abe? The Good Sisters of Charity personally told me that, if a person could tell just one lie (even a small one) to eliminate pain and suffering in the world, we could not do it because lying is wrong. As far as they were concerned, we must be honest, even if the truth hurts.

As devastating as it may sound, there is a time and place for everything, including the truth. This is not an advocacy statement for lying, but it is one for common sense. Certainly, when issues of personal integrity and one's credibility are at stake, there is no question that "honesty rules." For instance, a defendant who lies in a civil or criminal trial can be virtually assured a guilty conviction, even if the lie is about an insignificant matter. But, there are times when decisions about what to say and what not to say are not so clear cut.

How often are people offended or even alienated because they receive an honest answer to a relatively insignificant question like "Isn't my daughter pretty?" or "Do you like my outfit?" Get the picture? Often, in our personal life, we are not totally candid because it is not necessary to offend, criticize, or humiliate another person, even if these acts are done with honest statements. In fact, sometimes it is those honest statements that are the most hurtful. How about the blowhards who boast about always telling it like it is? If they really do, what motivates them to do it? And, if they are sensitive to the needs and feeling of others, would they have such a need for all this bravado? There are times when it is not necessary to be totally candid. In fact, it can be downright foolish or even dangerous to do so.

Leaders need to exercise discretion and common sense in their professional life, at least to the extent that they do in their personal life. Before answering any organizational question of importance, you must first determine if the questioner has a right to the answer. The second determination you must consider is the ramifications of the answer. On sensitive issues in which the questioner is entitled to an answer, the rule of thumb is to provide as little information as necessary to answer it—and nothing more. There are many ways to do this without being humiliating or embarrassing. Sometimes, being overly candid can cause more problems for the organization than a less candid response can. Any error in this regard should be caused by a restricted answer as opposed to an embellished one.

You must consider the consequences of being too blunt or too honest. There are times when answering a question or making an evaluative comment that people expect is both prudent and harmless. Chances are, those little white lies will not condemn you to eternal damnation and will be helpful to the organization. For instance, when a member shows you a picture of a Neanderthal-looking child and says, "Isn't Nanook beautiful?" your answer should be "Yes." Not "Are you blind?" On sensitive issues when a modified response is harmless, you must exercise common sense. There is a difference between honesty and diplomacy, and, at many times, discretion is the better part of valor.

Words are difficult to reclaim once they have been spoken and impossible to retrieve after they have been written. Prudence must be exercised in all forms of communication, but especially when you are speaking or writing responses to difficult questions. The cost of honesty could range from "thank you" to litigation. Treat others as you would prefer to be treated yourself is a good place to start. If you misspoke at a meeting, how would you accept criticism? If you made a bad suggestion, how would you like a leader to communicate your failure to you? It might not be okay to lie (although I might if it meant saving the world), but it certainly is allowable to hold back on criticisms, comments, and controversial statements to the level of dialogue that is necessary to make a point. Any more than that is overkill.

12. Be Attentive to Appearance and Personal Hygiene

Always present, but rarely addressed.

Leaders must be attentive to appearance and hygiene. Failure to comply with traditional norms of leadership dress and cleanliness will detract from the agenda the leader is attempting to advance. Halitosis, dirty fingernails, unkempt hair, body odor, stained and rumpled clothing, unwanted facial hair, and so forth neither fit the image of a leader nor engender respect and hero worship from the membership. Without good grooming habits, a leader's chances of being successful are greatly diminished. You should be a functional example of correctness, serving as a model for others to emulate. The scruffy look may be suitable for the captain of a men's soccer team after a contentious match, but, beyond that, it has limited appeal and is unworthy of someone in a leadership position.

Appearance

People respect uniforms. They want the policeman at the corner to wear his hat and badge. If a nurse assigned to the intensive care unit wears a halter top and jeans on duty, it makes patients and families less confident about the medical care they receive. How can Father O'Malley hear confessions without his Roman collar? What about that scandal Jimmy Carter caused when he wore jeans to a formal dinner party in France?

You are expected to wear the uniform of your leadership position. A stockholder attending a meeting for ABC Company (she owns 20,000 shares) expects Mr. CEO to be properly suited, and Ms. CEO to be the fashion plate of the female executive. In the 1950s, the expression was "clothes make the man." In contemporary society, the sentiment still prevails—without the gender bias, of course! With all due respect to the First Amendment to the Constitution, you must dress as your responsibilities dictate. Considering the variety of inappropriate outfits that people wear, the need for you to set a good example can never be overemphasized. The lower the standards are for the leader, the lower they are for the followers.

It is not surprising that the Dress Down Friday campaign is running its course. This little bit of social stupidity must have been a real windfall for Levis. From tie less men and skirt less women, the trend evolved into men in T-shirts and women without shoes. Employers are now demanding more for their salary buck; they want their employees back in uniform because it makes for better business and makes customers and clients more comfortable and much more respectful of the position. Dress counts!

What is appropriate dress? This topic is a book in itself. Fortunately, shelves of bookstores and public libraries are stocked with publications that specifically address this topic. You would be well-advised to research it in detail. Dress is recognized as an important form of communication. It has become a social science. It is a fact that specific attire elicits certain definitive types of human behaviors such as sexual desires (implicated by the color red) or calmness (associated with the color blue). Many corporate men have a closet full of "power ties." Dress influences human behavior (see Chapter 1), and, for this reason alone, you should always be properly attired in the uniform of the position.

Hygiene: Odors, Habits, and Whatever

Dirt and unpleasant odors detract from a leader's persona. The cosmetic industry spends a fortune each year to advertise toothpaste, deodorants, perfumes, aftershave cologne, and so forth. Each message (blatant or subliminal) reinforces the concept that clean, pleasant-smelling, manicured people experience greater acceptance than those who are not. This is an easy message to accept because it is true! Poor hygiene is a major turn-off that is rarely talked about. People are reluctant to tell a leader about his or her poor personal habits despite the damage this problem will cause to fulfilling the mission of the organization.

Halitosis

A contemporary radio advertisement for a vocabulary development product touts that "A poor vocabulary will sink you faster than bad breath." I doubt it! Let's have a reality check. Who would you be most likely to avoid: a person with a poor vocabulary or a person with bad breath? The former may make meaningful conversation difficult; the latter makes it intolerable. People avoid speaking with people with bad breath. This is not a minor issue; it can be a "deal breaker."

A leader with halitosis must correct it. Correcting it may be as simple as brushing one's teeth, using mouthwash, or employing any one of a number of over-the-counter products that are sold in any pharmacy. And, if the problem persists after corrective measures have been taken, it may signal the existence of a dental or medical problem that could have serious health ramifications requiring medical attention. In either case, halitosis cannot be ignored.

Body Odor

Body odor is another turn-off. People must bathe regularly using water and a mild soap. People who hide body odors by over applying perfume, deodorants, aftershave lotions, and similar products usually cause greater problems than the odors they attempt to mask. These man-made odors (regardless of how expensive they may be) can cause watery eyes, sneezing, and migraines in innocent bystanders. How many people do you know whose perfume announces their arrival and lingers long after their departure? Do you want to be remembered that way?

Daily bathing and a mild soap can usually correct a body odor problem. Washing one's hair on a regular basis cleanses the scalp of resident odors. There are many situations when a person is personally clean, but his or her clothing odor is offensive. In this case, washing or dry cleaning of clothes will keep them free of odor. Persistent body odor that defies all efforts to correct it can also be an indicator of an existing medical problem that should be investigated. The bottom line is that offensive odors must be eliminated.

The Barnyard Variety

There are also those grotesque sounds and odors that people intentionally or unintentionally emit—the "barnyard variety" of belches, burps, and flatulence. Ugh! There is a time and place for everything. If this is the case, bathrooms and open fields (when one is on a solitary walk) are much more appropriate than elevators, airplanes, cars, offices, churches, and first dates. Certain things should be kept to oneself. Stop blaming the dog!

Annoying Habits

Gum chewing, nail biting, sniffling, talking with food in one's mouth, smoking, and frequent blinking are just a few annoying personal habits that make it difficult for a leader to lead. They are a distraction to others. People want their leader to be a contemporary James Bond. He or she must be calm, cool, and collected. Popping gum, nail biting, or frantically blinking eyes suggest nervousness. Behind every nervous leader, there are a number of nervous followers, who become more apprehensive when they encounter their leader's annoying idiosyncrasies.

Correcting the Problem

Our human nature makes it difficult for us to tell another person that he or she smells, is dirty, or has a twitch that makes others uncomfortable or nervous. If there were ever a real test of your communication skills, this is it. However, for the well-being of the organization and the people involved, you cannot ignore these problems because they are serious impediments to the communication process. It is humanistic to help offending people become aware of their problem.

You must make it clear to a spouse, close friends, secretaries, and others in close working and social proximity that you want to be told if you have a recognizable problem. In turn, you must return the favor. There are times when everyone has the problems discussed in this chapter. A very late night followed by a very early morning can easily result in body odor, bad breath, disheveled hair, or wrinkled clothing. In these cases, it should be ignored. However, a recurring problem cannot be ignored; especially if these offensive problems are present before an important meeting or other equally as significant occasion.

In the final analysis, if it is too difficult for you to directly confront the offensive person for whatever the reason, send a copy of this section to him or her and sign it "With Love from a Friend."

13. Add a Twist of Theory X to a Full Cup of Sugar

The steel fist in the velvet glove

With every leader, even the more humanistic ones, a presence of strength must exist that is either spoken or implied. Behind the smile, enthusiastic reception, and openness of personality, people must recognize that you are determined to do whatever it takes to meet organizational goals. Members must realize you have high performance expectations and those who have organizational responsibilities will be held accountable. This is an important aspect of leadership. If the leader projects a timid and/or frightened image that suggests it is acceptable to be ignored, very few organizational goals will be met. Sometimes, applying Theory X is optional; at other times, it is a necessity.

Theory X: Revisited

The topic of management styles has been discussed in Chapter 2. Some components of Theory X have been paraphrased for your review. (For a full explanation, revisit Chapter 2.)

- ✓ The average human being dislikes and avoids work.
- ✓ Most people must be coerced, controlled, directed, and threatened with punishment to get them to put forth adequate effort.
- ✓ The average human being wishes to avoid responsibility.

Under specific circumstances, employing Theory X strategies to manage people will be successful in encouraging members to meet your performance expectations. Although fear is a negative motivator, there are circumstances when it will yield positive results.

Excuses, Excuses, Excuses

In today's hustle and bustle society, there are numerous demands on people's time. Family obligations, work assignments, social commitments, and so forth leave very few moments in which individuals can relax or catch up. Under pressure from several different directions, an individual will select the path of least resistance. If that path is to place the expectations of a hesitant leader on very low priority, then that is exactly what will happen. You cannot condone the behavior of members who place organizational priorities at the bottom of their to-do list. That person must rearrange priorities or be replaced by another who will be more responsive to organizational needs.

Gentleness is a wonderful quality in a perfect world, but there are times when your sensitivity is perceived as weakness. It is important that compassion and kindness not be interpreted as a signal to ignore your wishes. There must be consequences for:

- ✓ Failing to complete an assignment because of lack of effort
- ✓ Failing to follow through on organizational initiatives
- ✓ Ignoring or opposing organizational goals

Under these and/or similar circumstances, you must make it known you are a force to be reckoned with if it becomes necessary to do so. Fear of what you might do can serve as a deterrent to unacceptable membership performance.

Consequences of organizationally destructive behavior can range from your articulation of strong disappointment to the loss of that person's position of status in the organization to membership termination. As difficult as these actions may be to take, the failure of the leader to act when warranted is destructive to the entire organization because of the message of leadership weakness that is transmitted.

Yesterday's Wizard: Today's Spin Doctor

Remember the Wizard of Oz? Behind the big voice and intimidating smoke-screen was humanism personified. To some, the Wizard was feared; to others, he was revered. He was the quintessential example of both. The smoke and mirrors allowed him to accomplish whatever goals he needed, and, because of his bravado, he had never been challenged. Anticipation of what he might do was more horrifying than any action he could have taken. The Wizard was Theory Y hiding behind Theory X. If, like the Wizard, you establish a reputation of willingness to take action if the situation warrants it, it will deter others from behaving in a way that would call down your wrath. There are times when leaders must be Theory X hiding behind Theory Y.

In the final analysis, it is usually the lack of decisive action that causes members to become uncertain about the intent and commitment of their leaders. Justice, tempered with humanism, fairly and equally applied is a strong weapon for a successful leader.

14. Be Flexible

If it was good enough for my father, it's good enough for me!

Rigidity is the enemy of constructive leadership. In a forever-changing world, the astute leader must change with it. You must understand there are usually alternative solutions to any given problem, and you must be willing to consider new approaches to accomplishing the ends desired. However, despite the intellectual validity of this statement, emotionally, it is very difficult for us to accept. In fact, a major flaw in contemporary leaders is our reluctance to embrace alternative solutions to existing problems.

There is a certain comfort level in conducting business in the same old way. Idioms such as "If it ain't broken, don't fix it" are embedded in our contemporary style, and it defines one's life. Many leaders become stuck in a quagmire of resistance, and the concept of preventive maintenance goes by the wayside. They eventually fail because they cannot adapt with the times as they fight against new or alternative approaches to solving a problem or achieving an objective.

When computers came into widespread use, the opposition to them was enormous. Despite the obvious service this new and advanced technology could contribute to society, it represented change. To many leaders, computers denoted an uncharted excursion into the unknown. It required leaders to leave the familiar world and to enter one they did not understand and could not control. Many resisted. To them, it seemed easier to prevent society's growth than to grow with it.

But, resistance to change is not unique to contemporary leaders. It is inherent in man's nature and in his history. In the 1500s, the great Galileo was forced to recant his proofs that the world was round. Contemporary thinking at that time was that the world was flat. Inflexible religious leaders labeled Galileo's teachings as heresy. They silenced the message by hammering the messenger into submission, and scientific discovery was set back a hundred years. Galileo was not the first to be restricted by rigidity, and he will certainly not be the last. Today, similar efforts to prevent change are still being made at an alarming rate.

How often have positive, progressive movements been railroaded by people who were incapable of accepting alternatives to existing lifestyles? Inflexible leaders find any type of change to be extremely difficult and quite often impossible to accept. It took losing the Revolutionary War before colonial British officers were convinced there were alternatives to the unsuccessful ways they were fighting battles. How often have destructive behavioral patterns repeated themselves throughout history? If a police action failed in Korea, why did the United States think it would work in Vietnam? The Civil Rights Movement of the 1950s and the Women's Suffrage Movement at the turn of the century are examples of how human progress can be inhibited by the inflexibility of people who have the power to implement change and choose to oppose it instead. Fear of change and a desire to remain in a particular comfort zone often prevents good things from happening.

15. Solicit Constructive Criticism

The unachievable goal of great leadership is perfection

A leader must strive to be the very best and should work continually to achieve this end. Leaders should never become complacent with their job performance because complacency is another opponent of good leadership. Soliciting and being receptive to constructive criticism is an invaluable tool to help you move toward perfection. In doing so, it will help your organization to fulfill its mission.

Ed Koch was mayor of New York City from 1978 to 1989. Among politicians, he was the master of soliciting constructive criticism. As he wandered the streets of New York City, he would ask the passing pedestrians, "How am I doing?" He was loved for this openness and approachability. He understood that encouraging constructive criticism sends a message of interest and concern to one's constituents. It broadens the professional vision of the leader by as many extensions as there are people who are willing to respond truthfully to a legitimate request for information by a sincere leader.

Seeking the opinion of others will enable you to see those things that are not clearly in your direct line of sight, both figuratively and literally. Although there must be guidelines and processes in place as to when and how criticism is given and received, the validity of the process and the positive results from it cannot be emphasized enough.

The present national interest in self-evaluation has reached a frenzied level. People are asked to evaluate the quality of a hotel stay, the quality of food, and the quality of service at all types of consumer-friendly organizations. The list is endless! Automobile dealerships are persistent in seeking evaluations of their automobile service departments. Companies put their phone numbers on company-owned vehicles so that the performance of that vehicle's driver can be rated and reported to the company. Students are asked to evaluate their teachers; teachers are asked to evaluate their administrators. Nurses are asked about doctors; doctors are asked about the hospitals in which they work. The list is inexhaustible. Rumors have it that there is even a constructive evaluation system in place at the famous Bunny Ranch in Nevada. Sy Sims says, "An educated consumer is our best customer." People have not only become accustomed to being asked, "How am I doing?" they have become sophisticated enough to give honest answers to the questioner.

The primary purpose in soliciting constructive criticism is to improve performance. These evaluations can result in many enhancements ranging from changing one's behavior to introducing new technology. Any number of positive transformations can be the end product of a good self-evaluation system. There is clearly a direct relationship between improving productivity and improving customer satisfaction. Moreover, one of the ways to improve customer satisfaction is by asking the customer how and then implementing those recommendations that have merit.

You should request evaluative input from those you lead. Simply stated, you are the service provider, and your membership is the consumer. Seeking constructive criticism is no longer an optional exercise of leadership. It is something that every leader must do! The value of this process is beyond question. It is the fastest and most effective way to self-improvement and membership satisfaction. But it is also a process that requires you to put sensitivities aside and look at the benefits derived for the entire membership.

True, it is difficult to hear negative criticism of your performance. Yes, it is also difficult to hear statements of disappointment or failure. Our natural instinct is to become defensive and at times consider killing the messenger. Being receptive to constructive criticism is truly a challenge. But, by soliciting evaluative responses from those being served, you will inevitably learn of many more opportunities to advance the organization's mission.

A good leader gives and accepts constructive criticism. This willingness to accept input from constituents will make your evaluation of them more acceptable to members when they are the recipients of same. Your leadership sets the example. This process can begin with a suggestion box, improvement forums, satisfaction surveys, or with any other number of processes in which information is received and analyzed. Chapter 4 includes an evaluative tool, The Leader Meter that will provide you with a vehicle to assess leadership abilities as measured against the criteria listed in this book.

When you begin to solicit the opinions of those you lead and your membership realizes you are sincere in your request, the information you are requesting will be readily available. Members are always willing to help a leader to service the organization better. Improved performance is a win-win scenario for all those involved. Seeking constructive criticism and implementing valid suggestions should be on the to-do list of every leader.

16. Be a Go-To Person

The leader is the logical go-to person.

A leader must be viewed by an organization's membership not only as a problem solver but as a primary source of information and advice as well. The leader is not expected to know the answer to every question or provide the solution to every problem, but the leader is expected to be able to direct the membership to the resources that will help them. You must be the logical one to whom the members go. If an issue is important enough for your membership to be concerned about, it should also be important to you, regardless of how insignificant the matter might seem.

Accessibility

If members are expected to bring problems and concerns to you, then you or a designee must be accessible to the member. This is not possible all the time, especially in large organizations. But a system of communication must be in place so that a member's need is channeled to your attention accurately and quickly. This means that you must be accessible either directly or through someone who is in a position to forward information. The member should be notified their concern has reached you and of any pending action or disposition that is being contemplated. It is your responsibility to establish a network that provides an efficient flow of information both ways—from the membership to you as well as from you to the membership.

Understanding the Issue

Before you offer an answer to a question or a solution to a problem, you must fully understand the issue. Few things are more annoying to members than to receive an answer to the wrong question or a solution to a nonexistent problem. Even though you have a sincere interest in servicing the member, a breakdown in the processing of correct information sends a message of disinterest and indifference. Once you understand the nature and intent of the communication, you must ensure that it is addressed, either personally or through individuals to whom the issue has been delegated. This requires an understanding of the issue as well as having sufficient knowledge of the available resources to either resolve the issue or to refer the member to someone who can. However, at all times, you must keep the impacted member in the loop.

For instance, if a member requires legal information regarding an initiative that is being undertaken, it would be you or an intermediary who would provide the member with information about available legal services as well as the means of accessing them. Or, if a member needs additional resources to complete an assignment, you or the leadership team should make provisions for the member to get the needed resources.

The Go-To Information Booth

Many large department stores, corporate, state, and federal office buildings make availability and providing information a priority. Information booths are located in convenient locations for the intended purpose of helping visitors, clients, or customers locate or receive the services they require. Employees manning these booths know where offices and merchandise are located and the fastest way to reach every location. They have been trained to tend to the informational needs of whoever walks through the door.

Grand Central Station in New York City is a perfect example. The Information Booth is located in the middle of the action on the main level where train arrivals and departures are listed. The staff manning these booths can answer any question in their area of expertise without hesitation. They are there to help confused travelers, and they approach their job with a sense of reassuring confidence.

All organizations do not have the need and means to provide information booths. But, they do have to provide information in an accessible, understandable, and competent format. Information can be provided by a leader, an extremely knowledgeable staff member, and a comprehensive display of appropriate brochures, pamphlets, newsletters, advisory bulletins, or a well-developed Web site.

A good travel agency staffed with competent people provides an excellent model of the way information should be transmitted. There are few (if any) questions about travel and destinations that cannot be answered before a client leaves the office. Walls are lined with current brochures describing an endless variety of destinations, schedules of the various transportation options are at the agent's fingertips, and agents are on top of all relevant information regarding their industry and their clients' needs. If one agent cannot answer a question, another can. The entire office simulates the information booth that is so critical to their continued success.

You must be accessible to the membership. Whenever a member approaches the Go-To Leader with a question, problem, or a concern, that member expects an answer. A response such as "gee, I don't really know!" is unacceptable. "I'll get back to you as soon as I have an answer" is acceptable, but it is not as good as "I'll get back to you in an hour." The best response is for you to have an immediate solution or answer on the spot. The more knowledgeable you are about the organization and its needs, the more confident members are in your leadership.

Every organization must address leadership accessibility in a way that is relevant to that organization. This problem is not unique; it has been addressed, time and time again, by other organizations with similar goals. If you have not found a solution to this problem, investigate similar groups that have successfully resolved the issue of accessibility, and model your organization after one of them. However, the quest to finding a system to meet these needs must begin by realizing its importance.

Good leaders have their fingers on the pulse of the organization. Knowing does not mean micromanaging. It denotes dedication and concern. In addition, members know the leader is aware of and is interested in them and their work. This interest is infectious throughout the entire organization.

Chapter 3

General Responsibilities of Leadership

In a free society, countless opportunities are available for someone who wishes to be a leader to become one. Be it an organization as small as a neighborhood community association or as large as a Wall Street corporation, the need for people to fulfill leadership roles is endless. The pool of people who have the ability to lead is also very deep. But, despite this surplus of positions and existing need, many leadership positions go unfilled because people are reluctant to assume the responsibilities that come with them. The end product is that, in many sectors of society, positions remain vacant until an appropriate leader is found.

How a person is selected to lead depends on the sector of society in which the position exists. A student who attends a military academy such a West Point will be graduated into a leadership position in the military. In corporations, people are normally hired or promoted into positions. In service and social organizations, people are normally elected; others are appointed by those who have been elected. The titles affixed to leadership roles seem to be as endless as the leadership roles themselves. But, although leadership titles may differ from one sector of society to another, the general responsibilities are similar regardless of where in the hierarchical structure the position exists. Leadership is leadership is leadership…

The Motivated Leader

Leaders are distinctive because of their willingness to serve as well as their ability to do so. But a leader must want to lead! The reason a person chooses leadership may not necessarily be altruistic. Some will be motivated by the power the position offers. Compensation, release time, or country club dues may attract others. There are different stokes for different folks. However, within reason, if a person can meet or exceed the membership's expectations for a leader, it makes little difference why a person has accepted the call to lead. A candidate's motivations should not matter as long as the leader is capable and willing to fulfill the responsibilities of the position, operates within the law, and functions within the moral and ethical expectations of the organization.

The Reluctant Leader

On far too many occasions, people accept leadership positions because no one else will do it. These are usually kind-spirited individuals who find it hard to refuse a request for help or assistance. Although they are well-intentioned, they do a disservice to themselves as well as to the people they lead. An organization is poorly served by placing someone in a leadership position who does not want to be there.

The Accountability Factor

An organization should select a leader who wants the position. It is difficult to hold someone accountable for meeting the expectations of a leadership position when that person did not want it, did not choose it, and/or was coerced into accepting it. This being said, a leader must be prepared to accept the responsibilities of the position, and an organization must do whatever it can to make the role more appealing. Whether it is a salaried position or a stipend one, compensation validates an organization's right to hold a leader accountable. To a certain extent, "You get what you pay for." In today's world, it is not fair to expect an individual to serve continually in a leadership position without receiving some form of compensation.

The Chosen One

At the other extreme are the people who are so competent and so willing to lead that they become leaders in any activity in which they become involved. They become the captain of every team on which they play, the chairperson of every committee they join, or the president in every club in which they have a membership. Not only are these people frequently asked to lead, they thrive on the additional responsibility. However, their presence is so strong that it discourages others from stepping forward, even if they want the leadership position and are capable of succeeding in it.

The super leader must be discouraged from assuming multiple leadership positions. Not only does he or she dissuade others from stepping forward, but this super leader severely diminishes the opportunity for others to develop as leaders because they will not have the chance to cultivate their skills through experience and training. In addition, when the super leader decides not to or can no longer lead, vacancies in the respective positions become too difficult to fill because those organizations have not had the opportunity to groom replacements. Whenever it is possible to do so, assignment of leadership positions should be evenly distributed.

Commonality

The duties of a leader are as far-reaching and as varied as the organizations they lead. But, regardless of the specific position, meeting responsibility ultimately falls on the shoulders of the person leading. To paraphrase Harry Truman, the buck stops at that leader's desk. A corporate executive, for example, will be serving a different constituency than the president of a neighborhood garden club. But, there are common threads of leadership that are consistent across all organizational lines. This commonality is the focal point of this chapter.

1. Be a Cheerleader for the Organization

A major responsibility of leadership is to be the primary spokesperson that projects the public image of the organization. The leader must be a cheerleader as well as the captain of the squad!

On Monday evenings during football season, cheerleaders fill television screens with their cries of support and encouragement. They are positive, enthusiastic, and properly attired in the colors of their team. They encourage the crowd and the individual team members to achieve the organizational goal of victory. They work together, taking direction from their captain. They are there to support the team and are in synchronization with each other; they are both motivated and motivators. There is neither a question as to whom they support nor is there any doubt as to why they are there. In fact, a cheerleader who is not committed to supporting the team effort or is unenthusiastic is quickly dismissed.

Under the leader's stewardship, members encourage, support, and motivate each other to work collaboratively to achieve organizational goals. The captain's responsibility is to mentor and motivate the squad to work relentlessly until the mission has been successfully accomplished. The captain supports, badgers, and encourages the efforts of those who will assist in accomplishing the organizational goals.

As their leader, you must keep the membership focused on meeting its objectives. You are the parent, grandparent, brother, sister, confessor, and collaborator, all rolled up into one. You are the pivotal point in the organization and the primary organizational representative to whom members look to for clarification, support, and direction. You are the captain of the squad and must be the most enthusiastic cheerleader in the organization; you are the one who articulates its mission, its responsibilities, and its social worth.

2. Be a Visionary

If a man does not keep pace with his companions, perhaps, it is because he hears a different drummer. Let him step to the music he hears, however measured or far away.

—Henry David Thoreau

A leader must be philosophically in sync with the mission of the organization. You must assist your organization in developing goals, implementing plans, monitoring progress, and evaluating and reevaluating organizational initiatives. Your organization depends on you to give it direction and to help it stay focused. Part of that responsibility is to explore new and creative ways to assist members in maintaining interest and enthusiasm for the projects at hand.

It is your responsibility to fashion and implement those aspects of the plan that will help the organization stay on task. Your responsibility is akin to that of a tugboat captain steering his cargo on a stormy sea. The captain must anticipate problems and implement systems to overcome obstacles before they become major obstructions to sailing his boat into a safe harbor. This is his mission. Yours is to be the visionary who, like the captain, anticipates problems and overcomes obstacles to lead your organization to its safe harbor, that is, successful completion of its mission.

You must remain focused and not allow any break in the organizational concentration that would interfere with successfully completing the mission. As a visionary, you must constantly explore alternatives to help the organization complete its short- and long-term goals. For instance, if the undertaking is to raise money for a particular charity, you must be vigilant for new or innovative ways to raise the targeted funds. Or, if the mission is to build ten homes within a particular timeframe, it becomes your responsibility to implement those steps that are necessary to build those houses.

You are at the head of the organization; there should not be any doubt about who is in charge. You are not only the public image of the organization, but you also represent what it is. In most organizations, the mission is constant, but the approach to completing it need not be. Because the leader normally establishes the approach, it is imperative that you be a forward planner. Your vision will chart your organization's course.

3. Be a Teacher, Be a Learner

The educational aspect of leadership is extremely important to an organization. The leader must serve as an instructor, a counselor, and a mentor to the membership. A leader must also be a student who strives to remain current on all organizational concerns.

A Teacher

You must teach members about the history, philosophy, and goals of their organization. This fervor will help to build strong enthusiasm that is a necessity to being a successful organization. Instruction on procedures, bylaws, appropriate reporting techniques, and various managerial strategies is not only beneficial to the efficient operation of the organization, but it is also personally helpful to the individuals involved.

During your tenure, members will seek your advice on a variety of private and organizational matters. To many, especially the younger and less experienced members, you are a surrogate parent figure. Members will seek your help in solving difficult problems, and they will depend upon you to be a positive role model. Part of this responsibility is to counsel, support, and instruct on the various components of organization business. Explaining the reasoning behind a particular decision or providing advice on developing strong people management skills are all part of your instructional responsibilities.

Delegating responsibility is an excellent leadership tool; however, when you delegate, you must make accurate assessments about the capability of selected members to fulfill delegated assignments. Part of this assessment must be to determine if any mentoring is needed for a member to successfully complete a task. Frequently, leaders make false assumptions about a member's knowledge and/or ability and act upon those assumptions. Sometimes, in the spirit of collaboration and delegation, tasks are delegated to competent people who have not been properly prepared to carry out a specific assignment. They flounder because the leader has failed to accurately access their ability level and, therefore, not provided the needed training that would have turned a failed assignment into a successful one. You must be certain that those to whom you delegate have the proper recourses, including instruction, to successfully complete the assignment.

You also have a responsibility to identify members who have the potential to become future leaders in the organization. Once identified, you must provide them with leadership training in the form of instructing, mentoring, and monitoring. You must be an enthusiastic teacher to all who can benefit from your tutelage.

A Learner

In addition to being a teacher, you must be a learner. You must be willing to learn about any new factors that impact the organization and keep current on all matters of concern. In making a commitment to continued learning, you are also making a declaration of intent to be open-minded and approachable. The subtle message you transmit is that you are receptive to new learning. You are not asking the membership to do anything that you are not willing to do yourself.

This zest for knowledge also communicates enthusiasm and commitment. It is leadership by example. It shows the membership that you are willing to make thoughtful change that brings a sense of youthfulness and energy to an organization. Being an enthusiastic learner will help you to be an enthusiastic teacher. A symbiotic relationship exists between teaching and learning. Without both, there is neither. You have been chosen to lead because you have something beneficial to offer the organization. Sharing skills in a mentoring environment is all part of good leadership. Your responsibilities in these areas are significant:

First: To be a teacher and mentor.
Second: To be a continual learner
Third: To prepare capable members to assume leadership roles

4. Be a Positive Role Model

As the leader, you are held to a higher performance standard than the rank and file. You must be a role model, especially when the members are expected to comply with rules or complete tasks that they find distasteful. For instance, if you expect members to be punctual for meetings or appointments but then you arrive late, members will not take your expectations seriously. If committee reports are due at a specific time, but you ignore deadlines, this lowers the expectation level for everyone. And, if you insist on perfection for all written and spoken communications, the material that you produce had better be perfect.

The failure of the leader to follow organizational rules gives the membership license to do the same. The factory supervisor cannot declare the workplace to be a smoke-free zone and then wander through the plant smoking a cigar. Professional athletes cannot expect children to follow their message of being drug-free, smoke-free, or alcohol-free when they frequent bars, use steroids, and advertise for cigarette companies. And, parents who use illegal drugs will have a difficult time convincing their children of the inherent dangers of drug abuse. A leader with low self-performance expectations lowers the performance expectations for everyone else. "Do as I say, not as I do" does not work, especially in today's social climate.

In order to be followed enthusiastically, you must set and meet higher standards of performance and behavior for yourself than you do for your membership. Being the first to arrive on the job and the last to leave is not such a bad idea! Society, after all, expects the captain to be the last person to leave the ship.

This is not to say that you must be better than everyone else in performing a task; it is your positive efforts that will create higher standards for all. Accepting the responsibilities inherent in leadership and being held accountable for the overall performance of an organization is a primary responsibility of leadership.

Leadership is a 24/7 responsibility. People observe the leader and evaluate, praise, or criticize accordingly. All the qualities mentioned in this book are measured against a leader's performance every day. There are no timeouts. If one could pinpoint the single overriding component that influences an organization's success or failure, it would be the example set by its leader. When a leader sets a bad example, members seeking reasons not to perform do not have far to look to find them. The leader has provided them with the best excuse ever—they were only following the leader.

Years ago, a physical or moral deficiency in a national leader was concealed from the public. Babe Ruth was a drinker and womanizer, but this behavior was hidden from the millions of children who wanted to be just like the Babe. History classes never portrayed our founding fathers as anything less than god-like. Certainly, the promiscuity of many members of the clergy did not begin in the 1990s, but significant efforts kept these despicable acts from the general public. Why? Because members of the clergy represented a morality bar that society wanted to keep at the highest possible level. Do we really believe that Bill Clinton was the only president whose behavior in the White House was indiscreet?

In yesterday's puritanical world, the public at large understood the power of leadership by example and conspired with the media to keep those nasty little secrets, SECRET. The reason was easily understood. Impressionable children and adults follow the example of the leaders, either for good or for bad. The theory is that the followers of a do-gooder do good! But, the opposite is also true. Some followers use the poor example set by a leader to justify their own inappropriate behavior. A good leader leads by good example and, in that regard, is a positive role model.

5. Identify and Solve Problems

No organization is completely free of conflicts. From time to time, problems develop and require resolution. You must be an effective problem solver; organizations expect their leader to find solutions. The more expeditiously a problem is solved, the better it is for the entire membership. However, you cannot jump in with solutions before understanding the root issues. As a prerequisite for leadership involvement, you must ascertain the following:

First: That a problem actually exists
Second: A problem must be understood before initiating a solution.

Before intervening, you must separate fact from fiction. You cannot overreact or ignore issues that have a significant impact on the well-being of the organization. Only an impotent leader fails to address a problem. One who is indecisive and allows a conflict to fester beyond salvage renders the organization ineffective.

If there is a problem that requires you to intervene, you are expected to resolve it by using an intelligent, rational approach. In organizations in which systems are in place to address actual or potential problems, you must implement those procedures as prescribed. Where procedures do not exist, you must develop them.

The varieties of problems that can surface are as diverse as there are organizations. However, regardless of the organization, there are three categories that incorporate most organizational problems.

A. Problems caused by personality conflicts.

B. Problems caused by outside obstacles that impede organizational progress.

C. Problems caused by poor communication.

A. *Personality Conflicts*

Personality conflicts within an organization are universal and inevitable. Under the best of circumstances, among friends and comrades, there are times when personalities and egos interfere with the collaborative effort of the team. Even the most solemn and sacred of organizations have their conflicts. The Bible talks about conflicts among the twelve Apostles. "If it happens there, it can happen anywhere…" The existence of conflicts within an organization is not a criticism of leadership, but failing to address them is. Unaddressed problems can paralyze an organization.

Personality conflicts within the organization are the most common issues that a leader must contend with. Some are minor and can be worked out in a relatively short period of time; others are more pervasive and require a greater effort. It is during these times that the able hand of an astute leader must find common ground for all parties.

You should approach finding common ground for agreement in the following order:

1. The conflicting parties must be reminded of the organizational goals and their collective responsibility to work collaboratively to meet those goals. They must be encouraged to remain focused on the organizational needs as opposed to their own. It is your role to help them refocus, either by personally intervening or providing other interveners who may be better suited for this task.

2. Failing in efforts to get the feuding parties to refocus, your next step is to arrange a sit-down meeting among them to informally seek a resolution through mediation. If not you, you must select a person who is knowledgeable, objective, and skilled in the art of people management to accomplish this task. Once again, the primary purpose of the meeting is to encourage the parties to put aside their personal differences for the good of the organization. When compromise is possible, it should be negotiated as long as organizational goals are not altered or compromised.

3. If a decision must be made by you regarding the issue at hand, the best decision for the organization must take precedence. You must put personal friendships, animosities, and preconceptions aside.

4. If all else fails, you must change staffing, either within the committee where the conflict exists or within the entire organization. Whatever the decision, meeting the goals of the organization must be the primary focus. At no time should you allow personalities and petty conflicts to jeopardize the fulfillment of the mission.

B. *Remove Obstacles*

Obstacles that interfere with meeting organization goals must be removed or circumvented. If it is a matter of insufficient funding, you must either establish ways to acquire the necessary monies or find less expensive ways to meet the established goals. If people are the cause of the interference, you must work collaboratively with others to remove or work around this impediment. If it is a time management problem or an insufficient staffing problem, you must find or allow others to find solutions to these problems.

However, assigning others to the task does not release you of ultimate responsibility in these matters. If you have assigned a person a task who does not have the ability to successfully complete it, you must replace that person with someone who does. If more time, staff, or resources are legitimately needed to get the job done and if the goal is realistic and worthwhile, then you must address these needs head on and make the necessary adjustments. This requires you to be current on the activities and needs of the organization.

C. *Resolve Communication Problems*

For the sake of clarification, the word communication is used in this section to refer to the processing and transmission of information of any kind by any vehicle including—but not limited to—speech, writing, smoke signals, telephones, signing, and the like. The purpose of this section is not to provide instruction on how to use various components to communicate more effectively. Volumes of material are available in every library to assist in the development of specific skills in specific areas. This section is intended to emphasize that poor communication in any form is a problem that cannot be ignored.

A breakdown in communications often causes organizational failures. Failure to communicate clearly and efficiently creates more problems in an organization than any other issue. This is not only embarrassing to a leader; it can undermine the workings of the entire organization as well. The more efficiently an organization communicates, the more successful that organization will be.

Communication problems exist in all organizations, regardless of their size. At the national level, investigations surrounding 9/11 have clearly identified a failure of intergovernmental agencies to exchange vital information as being at the root of this country's failure to anticipate and prevent that heinous crime. On the battlefield, deaths as a result of friendly fire have numbered in the thousands. Historians speculate that even Pearl Harbor could have been avoided had it not been for severe communication lapses among the various components of government.

Closer to home, parents do not communicate with their children, schools do not communicate with parents, and governments do not communicate with their constituents. Teenagers complain they are not understood, and fathers complain they do not have enough information to understand. The list is inexhaustible. The failure to communicate on a global basis is at the root of many catastrophes facing mankind.

It is common sense that, if poor communication causes problems, then it must become your primary responsibility to ensure good communication. Unfortunately, because this problem is thought to be indigenous to mankind, most leaders accept it and attempt to work around it instead of facing and correcting it head on. The usual outcome is that failed communication systems replace failed communication systems as human error and indifference renders each new system ineffective. Apathy and circumvention are not the solution. The solution lies in investigating and in being persistent in implementing corrective steps in each and every place where breakdowns occur.

The Solution: Investigate, Repair/Replace, Test, Monitor, Evaluate

Whenever and wherever a communication problem surfaces, regardless of its size, it must be investigated and corrected—traced from its root through the existing chaos until it is found. Next, you must be put a system in its place that will ensure clarity and structure. The replacement process must be tested, monitored, and evaluated. Depending on the size and structure of the organization, you might consider placing a specific member in charge of communications with the responsibility and authority to maintain, correct and make all necessary changes to the existing system as problems occur.

Your priority must be to establish flawless organizational communications. You should view the correction process as being similar to that of a lineman in a phone company who has been assigned to find and repair the broken line. The repair agent traces the line from its origin, and, when the break has been discovered, it is repaired/replaced and then tested. In any organization, each communication problem must be systematically traced, solved, and tested in a similar fashion with appropriate monitoring steps to ensure correction during and after the change has been completed. The seriousness of communication problems cannot be emphasized enough, but failure to achieve a goal or complete an assignment should never be caused by a problem that is traced to a bad communication network.

6. Ensure Organizational Efficiency and Stability

For an organization to fulfill its purpose, it must have structure, direction, and stability. Members feel secure in knowing there is a purpose in their membership and there is an organizational format that establishes a hierarchy for supervision, decision making, and accountability. They need to know someone is in charge and there is a system in place for evaluating and revising organizational goals. Chaos within an organization creates disharmony and instability that will undermine the entire operation.

Efficiency

An organization has serious problems when members are unable to get answers to reasonable questions, when format and structure are absent, when definitive action has been replaced by inactivity, and when it is evident that there is no forward progress. A leader must establish and adhere to a workable operational framework that gives the membership a clear and understandable direction. Failing to do so causes organizational mayhem.

Of course, it is not possible for you to have a plan for every action or initiative all the time. There are times when unpredictable events occur that cause the alteration of even the most detailed plan. Flying by the seat of one's pants from time to time is inevitable. In fact, good leadership expects the unexpected. But, when the unexpected becomes the routine, it is indicative of chaotic leadership that impedes membership productivity. In chaos, there is inefficiency. Inefficiency means that time and valuable resources are wasted. It also reflects poorly on you. Inefficiency at the top eventually permeates and negatively impacts every aspect of the organization.

Organizations require plans, structures, goals, and various lines of responsibility from the top down to the bottom up. With each initiative, you must anticipate results and incorporate checkpoints along the way to ensure the plan is implemented. You must replace confusion with clarity. Lack of direction must be replaced by an organizational blueprint that establishes a mission and a course of action. Duplication of efforts must be replaced by task reassignments. Failure to communicate adds to the chaos and must be replaced by a program that lets the right hand know what the left hand is doing. The more detailed the direction given, the less chance there will be of deviating from the path being followed. Members must know what they are expected to do.

Thomastic philosophers once debated the question, "How many angels can fit on the head of a pin?" After hours and hours of useless debate, the bottom-line answer was always, "No more or less than what is required to do whatever job has to be done." Organizations must function under the same philosophical premise. Duplication of assignments without a specific purpose for doing so only adds to the confusion.

Insuring Stability

One of the more successful ways to insure stability and avoid chaos is to develop a membership team. This is a small number of organization members who share in the decision making process and are kept current on all aspects of the organization. Team members are chosen for a number of reasons, but the most significant one is that they have skills that compensate for leadership weaknesses in specific areas. [This team has an entirely different purpose than the Internal Communication Network (ICN) that has been addressed in a previous chapter.]

For instance, suppose your organization requires interaction with other organizations in which English is not the spoken language. A chosen member of the team would be someone who is fluent in the second language if you are not. Alternatively, suppose your organization requires interaction with people whose mores and customs differ substantially from the mainstream American. In this case, a person possessing extensive knowledge of that culture would be an ideal member of the team.

The intent of a managerial team is to provide you with another level of expertise by members with different backgrounds and experiences. Shared decision making adds to organizational stability on a daily basis and assists in the unimpeded development of an organization's long-term plan. In stability, there is efficiency; in efficiency, there is stability. It is your responsibility to ensure that both are present in all aspects of an organization's development.

7. Monitor, Assess, and Supervise

When developing organizational goals, you must ensure they are reasonable and attainable. Once finalized, goals must be followed by developing specific plans to implement them. The merits of each goal should be revisited and reassessed regularly. Simultaneously, you must continually move the organization toward goal completion. For example, a goal might be to increase membership by ten percent within a calendar year or reduce annual spending by $5,000. In both cases, a plan to implement each goal within the designated timeline should be developed and followed until completed, changed, or aborted.

A leader also has a responsibility to give the organization a candid assessment of its initiatives and a prognosis for their outcomes. There will be times when your opinion will be based upon an objective analysis. At other times, it will be based upon intuition, that is, that sixth sense that gives direction to actions that are not clearly delineated and frequently referred to as hunches. It is vital that, when you are rendering an assessment, you identify whether it is based upon fact or that sixth sense. Upon organizational reaffirmation the goal selected is to be pursued, it is your responsibility to pursue it, regardless of your personal feelings about its merits.

Your leadership responsibilities in these areas are significant. The members you assign to implement plans must be helped, trained, supported, praised, or corrected as needed. Successful workers should be praised; poor workers should be replaced by others who can do the job. All projects must be reassessed, supervised, and evaluated regularly. An organization has a right to rely upon the honesty, forthrightness, ability, and professionalism of its leader.

8 Maintain Good Relationships

> *"God made us sisters…Prozac made us friends."*
>
> —Anonymous

The leader is the soul, spirit, and voice of an organization. A leader mirrors the organization and reflects what it is and what it is not. Unless the organization is located in a monastic convent in the Himalayas and does not require outside contact, from time to time, that organization will have to interact with other groups. Therefore, it is imperative that you maintain good relationships with all components with whom the organization may interrelate. The stronger and more harmonious the ancillary relationships are, the greater the benefit to the organization.

The Diplomat and Dr. Jekyll

Diplomats have made a living out of cultivating and capitalizing on social and professional relationships. Clearly, the absence of confrontation and contentiousness enables reasonable people to resolve difficulties in a civilized manner. Diplomacy opens doors that may normally be shut and provides an opportunity for productive communication. Harmony provides a better opportunity for cooperation and collaboration than confrontation. It is the role of the leader to build bridges, not destroy them.

If you are not a trained diplomat or do not possess an extremely high level of self-control, being ambassadorial under stressful circumstances can be a challenging, if not an impossible assignment. It is difficult to be tolerant when your counterpart is demeaning and combative. It is very hard to preach cooperation when you are faced with people who are abusive and refuse to cooperate. Moreover, it is difficult to remain honest when confronted with blatant and unbridled dishonesty. However, you must be strong, honest, decisive, principled, and always polite, gracious, and willing to see the other side of issues. To some, this cooperative, not confrontational spirit is weakness, but, in actuality, it is strength. It requires a leader to use power in a different way. However, turning the other cheek is not as easily accepted in practice as it is palatable in theory.

Remaining calm and collective can be difficult, but this is exactly what is expected of you. You must set aside your personal differences, negative feelings, and hostilities for the sake of the organization. A classroom teacher or administrator who, out of exasperation, shouts at a student to "Get the hell out of here" will spend more time explaining those actions than in addressing the child's unacceptable behavior that caused the outburst in the first place. The teacher is not expected to behave like the child. The same is true for leaders. You cannot behave like the buffoons who are the cause of the irritation.

The fewer your professional enemies, the less conflict there will be for the organization. If you are considered to be difficult, confrontational, or belligerent, the consequences for your organization will not be good. In fact, it may well become a major impediment to achieving organizational goals. There may be times when you have to walk a fine line between conflict avoidance and compromising the organization. In these situations, you must be the diplomat who can walk that line and negotiate a resolution to sensitive issues without making concessions that hinder your mission.

Hello, Mr. Hyde

The closing comment on the topic of maintaining good relationships may appear to be contradictory to what has preceded it. But, there are times when, if all else fails, there must be an iron fist in the velvet glove. If you have to go beyond the point of reasonable tolerance in an attempt to be conciliatory, you will be perceived as being weak. This perception will be harmful to the organization. There is a point in time when being collaborative, conciliatory, gentle, and compassionate must be balanced with a seriousness of purpose and a projection that, if you are pushed beyond a tolerable point, there will be unpleasant consequences.

Everyone knows wonderful people who they never want to anger. There is a bit of Mr. Hyde in all of us—or there should be. This is a message that you must also communicate. People must know that, if their behavior provokes you, they will meet your Mr. Hyde. Your strength as a leader might initially be measured by the words you speak, but it will be eventually measured by your actions and accomplishments. As your track record reflects your ability, you will face fewer challenges to your leadership.

Joe Louis, the great heavyweight boxing champion, was gentle. Yet, no one wanted to get him angry, so he never had to lose his temper, raise his voice, or make idle threats. His reputation identified the parameters for anyone who wanted to have a relationship with him. A good leader can also be a gentle giant. Martin Luther King Jr. was not a violent man, but his strength was undeniable. President Theodore Roosevelt offers all leaders sage advice for all ages, "Speak softly and carry a big stick."

The Art of Disagreement

Leaders need to practice the art of agreeing to disagree. A leader has a mission. Some people will support you and assist in the completion of that mission; others will not. In fact, others may even work against its successful completion. That is all part of leadership. Seldom is opposition meant to be a personal affront. If this were the case, every athletic competition or professional debate would end in a brawl. In most cases, the basis of conflict is honest disagreement. By focusing on the mission, you will avoid conflicts about what may appear to be personal matters but are actually impersonal.

Respecting another's position or beliefs on an arguable issue will help you to understand it. Understanding the issue from all points of view is the first step in bringing about compromise, agreement, or change. One thing is certain. As soon as you lose self-control, you have lost. Members expect their leaders to be objective, rational, and diplomatic.

9. Maintain Good Health

The necessity for a leader to be in good personal health is something that is often not addressed. Nevertheless, good health is an integral part of good leadership and cannot be ignored. Although detailed advice in this area should be left to the medical profession, certain truisms must be mentioned.

Too often, the pressures of leadership cause leaders to unintentionally abuse their bodies. These difficulties can range from not getting enough sleep to attending social functions in which rich foods and alcohol are readily available and easily consumed. The pressures that are part of leadership can be extremely dangerous to an undisciplined person. It is incumbent upon you to take whatever steps are necessary to avoid activities, foods, and functions that are unhealthy and/or dangerous. It is a responsibility that you have to yourself, your family, and your organization.

It is extremely difficult to operate at peak performance when you have serious health problems. It is vital for you to do whatever is necessary to stay physically fit. Leaders who do not take care of their own health needs are ill-equipped to take care of the needs of others. At the very least, you should have annual physicals and follow the advice of the physician performing the evaluation. Clearly, issues that can lead to debilitating diseases or worse should be given your immediate attention. Beyond that, you should make a commitment to living a healthy life that is free of recreational killers, such as drugs or tobacco. On this point, the wisdom of Socrates is paramount, "A sound mind in a sound body."

Finally, poor health causes absenteeism, which can eventually lead to chaos and doubt. Members not only expect you to be healthy, they expect you to look healthy. You must appear to be capable of beating down opposition if it ever became necessary to do so. For the membership, it is a matter of perception, confidence, and trust. You must make your personal health your first responsibility.

Chapter 4
The Leader Meter

Many aides are available to develop strong leadership skills; introspection is one. Another is the value of being receptive to constructive criticism, regardless from whence this criticism might come.

The Leader Meter has been designed to mirror the various aspects of this book. It will help you measure actual performance against those criteria as part of a self-assessment process. In each category, you are asked to self-rate on a scale of 1 through 5. The ratings are as follows:

5 = EXCELLENT
4 = GOOD
3 = FAIR
2 = POOR
1 = NONEXISTENT

✓ Once your self rating is completed, you should duplicate this questionnaire and seek validation from several individuals (approximately ten to twenty) who would be willing to objectively and anonymously evaluate you according to the same criteria. The larger the sample is (within reason), the greater the validity.

✓ Compare the findings (i.e., average the scores of each item) against your self-evaluation.

✓ In cases in which scores are identical, you should develop a self-improvement plan for each area in which the score is 3 or less. In areas in which outside evaluators differ significantly from yours, the findings of the evaluators should be treated as valid, and your findings should be ignored. Low-score areas are indicative of areas in which you must design and follow a self-improvement plan.

✓ It is important that you do not try to improve everything at once. A slow, steady, and consistent pace, addressing a few items at a time is the way to proceed and succeed.

✓ At the end of six months, retest by following the same process. Based upon the results at that time, reconstruct your improvement plan according to the same guidelines outlined in Chapter 5. However, this time, the outside evaluators should be different.

✓ Improving in areas of weakness requires a commitment and an awareness of the necessary steps to take to reach the desired end. The more familiar you are with the various methods of self-improvement as outlined in Chapters 1-3, the more successful you will be in turning weaknesses into strengths.

✓ Follow the Leadership Development Plan as outlined in Chapter 5. Practice, believe in yourself and positive change will happen.

IT IS TIME TO BEGIN!

THE LEADER METER

Score	Nonexistent 1	Poor 2	Fair 3	Good 4	Excellent 5
Chapter 1: The Right Stuff					
Has Credibility					
Is Honest					
Has Integrity					
Is Patient					
Is Organized					
Communicates Effectively					
Overall Performance					
Speech: Formal					
Informal					
Writing: Formal					
Informal					
Listens					
Body Language					
Appearance					

Score	Nonexistent 1	Poor 2	Fair 3	Good 4	Excellent 5
Chapter 1: *The Right Stuff (continued)*					
Makes Decisions					
Good Sense of Timing					
Knows When to Hold and Fold					
Empowers Members					
Supports Members					
Is Secretive					
Is Confidential					
Is a Risk Taker					
Recognizes Others					
Leads by Good Example					

Score	Nonexistent 1	Poor 2	Fair 3	Good 4	Excellent 5
Chapter 2: *The Leader's To-Do List*					
Is Self-Confident					
Articulates a Philosophy					
Understands the Organization					
Accepts Responsibility					
Understands Limitations					
Articulates a Plan					
Effective at Running Meetings					
Builds Consensus					
Is Objective					
Effectively Delegates					
Is Honest but Prudent					
Is Discrete					
Is Well-Groomed					
Is Flexible					
Solicits Constructive Criticism					
Is Approachable and Available					

Score	Nonexistent 1	Poor 2	Fair 3	Good 4	Excellent 5
Chapter 3: *The Responsibilities of Leadership*					
Supports Organization					
Is a Visionary					
Is a Teacher					
Is a Learner					
Is a Positive Role Model					
Is a Problem Solver					
Removes Obstacles					
Resolves Communication Problems					
Ensures Organizational Stability					
Is Efficient					
Effectively Supervises					
Evaluates Progress					
Maintains Good Relationships					
Maintains Good Health					

Chapter 5
Constructing Your Leadership Development Plan

At this point you have studied the qualities and characteristics of good leadership, identified those tasks that a leader must attend to and reviewed the overall responsibilities of the office. The final step is to put this information together in a meaningful way that will help you to achieve your leadership goals. It is time to develop your individualized plan to become a successful leader.

Your Trip Tik to success

Begin by reviewing the objective data you have already collected. Analyzing this information will help you to assess the quality of your current level of leadership skills and to determine the areas where there are weaknesses. Two valuable pieces of information that are available to you are:

- ✓ The Good and Bad Leader Inventory that you constructed after reading the Introduction to this book.
- ✓ The information you accumulated from the Leader Meter assessments you completed after reading Chapter 4.

The way you were

Your Good and Bad Leader Inventory defines your beliefs about what constituted good leadership before you read this book. It is now time to challenge your prior beliefs. Take a few moments to revisit your inventory and consider the following questions:

- ✓ Were the negative experiences you listed as bad as you remembered them to be?
- ✓ Would you still take the same steps to turn those negatives into positives?
- ✓ Were your positive experiences really that good?
- ✓ If so, were they positive for the right reasons?

✓ Have your beliefs about good leadership been validated?

✓ Have you changed your thinking about what constitutes good leadership?

✓ Have you concluded that there is more to leadership than what you originally thought?

✓ If so, what is different?

The Leader Meter and your Plan

Analyze the results of the Leader Meter, both yours and the assessments that others have made about you.

✓ Have your self-determined strengths and weaknesses been validated by others?

✓ Is there a consensus on your weak points?

For instance, suppose you identified this weakness of a prior leader, that is, he was not a details person. But, the Leader Meter assessment by others rated you as also performing poorly in the related skills of being organized and delegating. Your Inventory indicates that you consider these skills to be important, but others whom you trust say you are lacking in them. This is a strong indicator these are skills that you must improve upon.

In a similar manner determine the average score you received by others on every item listed in the Leader Meter. Compare each item assessment to your self-assessment. This will help you to determine whether others see you as you see yourself.

On a separate sheet of paper, list every item in which a consensus score on the Leader Meter is a 3, 2, or 1. When in doubt, add the item to the **Random List**, even though there may not be a consensus. As you list these items, do not attempt to put them into any specific order. Identifying and listing the items is critical to the developmental process, but attempting to rank them at this stage inhibits this procedure and will be counterproductive. Your immediate goal is to establish a comprehensive list of items that need improvement, nothing more. This is an imperfect science; you need not be too precise.

Heading to the Finish Line

At this point, you have a **Random List** of qualities, skills, areas lacking knowledge, and things you must teach yourself. Although Leader Meter assessments are subjective, consensus scoring and the listing of items are objective. If the item is a 3, 2, or 1, it belongs on the **Random List**, regardless of your personal feelings about it. When you have completed this step, review it one more time. It is important that nothing is omitted. You now have everything lined up properly to finalize your Plan.

1. Begin by dividing your paper into four columns, heading each column as shown in the chart below entitled **Initial Chart**.

2. Drawing from your **Random List** of weak skills (3, 2, 1), place every item that appears on it into one of the four columns on your **Initial Chart**. These column headings represent Qualities and Skills, Items you must learn, Items you must learn to do, and Items you must do.

For example, suppose your **Random List** of twelve items appears below.

Random List of items scoring 3–2- or 1

Item	Leader Meter Score
Hygiene	3
Patience	1
Learn about Organization	1
Build Consensus	3
Plan	1
Discretion	2
Philosophy	3
Get Organized	2
Run Meetings	1
Assessment	2
Empower	3
Credibility	3

Place each item from the **Random List** into **one** of four columns as indicated below. **Do not duplicate items by placing one or more items into several columns.** Your **Initial Chart** will look like this.

Initial Chart			
Column 1	2	3	4
Qualities & Skills	Learn About	Learn How to	Must Do
Patience (1)	Lrn Organization (1)	Run Meetings (1)	Hygiene (3)
Credibility (3)	Philosophy (3)	Build Consensus (3)	Empower (3)
Discretion (1)	Assessment (2)	Plan (1)	Get Organized (2)

Using your **Initial Chart**, treat each column as a separate entity, prioritize each list in each column by placing those rated as 1 at the top, followed by 2s and 3s in that order. Your **Revised Chart** might look like this:

Revised Chart			
Column 1	2	3	4
Qualities & Skills	Learn About	Learn How to	Must Do
Patience (1)	Lrn Organization (1)	Plan (1)	Get Organized (2)
Discretion (1)	Assessment (2)	Run Meetings (1)	Empower (3)
Credibility (3)	Philosophy (3)	Build Consensus (3)	Hygiene (3)

Finally, The Plan

This evolving list becomes your *Trip Tik* to self-improvement.

In each column, select the top item and place it into a column entitled Project List (see Column 5 below).

Do not attempt to improve all items at the same time; concentrate on one item from each column simultaneously. For instance, on the above list, it would be difficult to focus on Learning to Plan (Column 3) and Build Consensus (Column 3) at the same time, but it is relatively easy to concentrate on one item from each column, for example, Patience (Column 1), Learning about the Organization (Column 2), Planning (Column 3), and Getting Organized (Column 4), simultaneously because each require a distinctly different approach.

Column 5	Found In
Project List	
Patience	Column 1
Learn about the Organization	Column 2
Plan	Column 3
Get Organized	Column 4

Do not work on any other item in a specific column until you have established a proficiency in the top item in that column. In other words, using above examples, do not attempt to master Building Consensus (Column 3) if you are still working on Planning (Column 3). You can always be working with four items at the same time, but each item must be from a separate column.

The Project List

The **Project List** is made up of the items listed at the top of each of the other four columns on your **Initial List**. This list becomes your map. Your Plan is to improve each item and then replace it with another item from its same column.

Thus, using the **Revised Chart**, upon mastery, Discretion would replace Patience (Column 1); Assessment would replace Organization (Column 2) etc. If you require additional information on any item, *The Common Sense Guide to Leadership* becomes your initial reference book.

In your Plan, you must incorporate periodic assessments to monitor your progress. You may think you have mastered "Running Meetings," but that does not make it so. Become an Ed Koch, and ask others, "How am I doing?" When you have earned a rating of 4 or higher on a specific skill, replace it in the **Project List** with another from the column from whence it came. Within a reasonable period of time, all of your Leader Meter scores will be in the 4s and 5s. You will be a good leader.

To achieve greatness, revisit the entire process. Place all of your 4s in each respective column, prioritize, and work them the same way you worked the 1s, 2s, and 3s. Just keep working hard on it. Good things come to those who persevere.

Chapter 6
My Ending—Your Beginning

The Common Sense Guide to Leadership has familiarized you with many tools that will:

- ✓ Teach you about the qualities and skills you will need to be a successful leader
- ✓ Help you to focus on what good leadership is
- ✓ Enable you to identify your strengths and weaknesses as a leader

You mission is to become a successful leader. You have the determination and the self-confidence to succeed, and now you have your Plan. Success is at your doorstep.

A Sidebar

Building good leadership skills is part of a developmental process. It takes time and practice. It is analogous to running in a marathon race, as opposed to a sprint. You must prepare and pace yourself accordingly. Throughout this book, I have emphasized that leadership is an acquired skill, but I never said it was acquired easily or quickly. You must be patient, work hard, and follow your Plan.

Learning is a process of identification, repetition, practice, introspection, and self-evaluation. Remember when you first learned to drive a car? If you attempted to do everything the manual and your instructor tried to teach you on your first outing, you probably would not have lived long enough to talk about it. You learned to drive by taking it step-by-step. When you mastered one step, you continued to practice it while you concentrated on another. Eventually (and safely), you became a proficient driver.

Most of the information we acquire and the skills we learn throughout our life, we develop sequentially. Frequently, there are negative consequences whenever we skip a step in this evolutionary process. This is why educators become alarmed when they learn that a child walked without crawling; they know that skipping this important step might impede a child's later ability to do many things well, including reading. Becoming a good leader (good first, great later) is a long-term goal. There aren't any shortcuts. A prerequisite for success is your patience as the process evolves.

Happy Trails

I have been a successful leader for almost forty years. Each position had its own set of challenges; each offered a unique set of rewards. Throughout my entire career, the guidelines that I have provided in *The Common Sense Guide to Leadership* have helped me at every step along the way, regardless of the position I was holding. It has served me well, and it will serve you equally so. I can think of no better way to serve mankind than to lead others in the right direction. Being a successful leader is incredibly fulfilling and personally rewarding. You are well on your way to experiencing the exhilaration that successful leadership affords you.

Written on the auditorium wall above the stage in the building where I served my first high school principalship is the following statement, "Work is God's Gift to Man." To those words, I would add, "Leading Others is Your Gift to Mankind." Your time is now. Carpe Diem! Good luck and "Happy Trails to you…"

Bibliography

Artz, Frederick. *The Mind of the Middle Ages*. Chicago: The University of Chicago Press, 1980.

Bagin, Don, and Donald R. Gallagher. *The School and Community Relations*. Boston: Allyn and Bacon, 2001.

Bailey, Edward J. Jr., Philip A. Powell, and Jack M. Shuttleworth. *The Practical Writer: Paragraph to Theme*. New York: Holt, Rhinehart, and Winston, 1979.

Boorstin, Daniel J. *The American: The Democratic Experience*. New York: Vantage Books, 1974.

Brereton, John C. *A Plan For Writing*. New York: Holt, Rhinehart, and Winston, 1978.

Cantor, Norman F. *The Civilization of the Middle Ages*. New York: HarperCollins Publishers, 1993.

DiLorenzo, Thomas J. *The Real Lincoln*. California: Prima Publishing, 2002.

Donovan, Timothy R., and Ben W. McClelland, eds. *Eight Approaches To Teaching Composition*. Illinois: National Council of Teachers of English, 1980.

Ellis, Joseph J. *Founding Brothers*. New York: Alfred A. Knopf, 2000.

Fast, Julius. *Body Language*. New York: M. Evans and Company Inc., 1970.

Foerster, Norman, ed. *American Poetry and Prose*. Boston: Houghton Mifflin Co., 1952.

Fullan, Michael. *Leading in a Culture of Change*. California: Jossey-Bass, 2001.

Gephardt, Richard. *Floor Speech on Impeachment*. Washington, D.C.: Associated Press, 1998.

Goldman, Daniel. *Primal Leadership*. Boston: Harvard Business School Press, 2002.

Goleman, Daniel. *Emotional Intelligence*. New York: Banton Books, 1995.

Guralnik, David B., ed. *Webster's New World Dictionary: Second College Edition.* New Jersey: Prentice Hall, 1972.

Harari, Oren. *The Leadership Secrets of Colin Powell.* New York: McGraw-Hill, 2002.

Harvey, Paul. *The Oxford Companion to English Literature.* Oxford: Clarendon Press, 1967.

Humes, James C. *Churchill: Speaker of the Century.* New York: Stein and Day, 1980.

Jessup, Michael H., and Margaret A. Kiley. *Discipline: Positive Attitudes for Learning.* New Jersey: Prentice Hall, Inc., 1971.

Kraut, Richard. *The Cambridge Companion to Plato.* New York: Cambridge University Press, 1992.

McGregor, Douglas. *The Human Side of Enterprise.* New York: Mc-Graw-Hill Co., 1960.

McNergney, Robert F., and Joanne M. Herbert. *Foundations of Education: The Challenge of Professional Practice.* Boston: Allyn and Bacon, 2001.

Miller, Nathan. *F.D.R: An Intimate History.* New York: Doubleday & Company, Inc., 1983.

Molloy, John T. *John T. Molloy's New Dress For Success.* New York: Warner Books,1988.

Morris, Edmond. *The Rise of Theodore Roosevelt.* New York: Ballantine Books, 1979.

New York State School Boards Association. *School Law: 28th Edition.* New York: New York State School Boards Association, 2000.

Nierenberg, Gerard I., and Henry H. Calero. *How to Read a Person Like a Book.* New York: Hawthorn Books, Inc., 1971.

Nixon, Richard. *Leaders.* New York: Warner Books Inc., 1982.

Ouchi, William. *How American Business Can Meet The Japanese Challenge.* New York: Avon Books, 1993.

———. *Theory Z.* New York: Avon Books, 1982.

Peter, Laurence, J. *The Peter Principle.* New York: Banton Books, 1984.

Rogers, Carl R. *On Becoming a Person*. Boston: Houghton Mifflin Co., 1989.

Senge, Peter M. *The Fifth Discipline*. New York: Currency Doubleday, 1990.

Shaafa, Jeff. *Rise To Rebellion*. New York: Ballantine Books, 2001.

Shaafa, Jeff. *The Glorious Cause*. New York: Ballantine Books, 2002.

Smith, Denis.Mack. *Mussolini*. New York: Alfred A. Knopf, 1982.

Wainwright, Gordon R. *Teach Yourself Body Language*. London: McGraw-Hill, 2003.

ORDER FORM

Fax Orders: 914-576-3461   Phone Orders: 914-637-9021
E-mail: jfscsi@msn.com

Postal Orders: JFS CONSULTING SERVICES INC.
24 Skyview Lane
New Rochelle, NY 10804

Please send me _____copies of <u>The Common Sense Guide to Leadership</u>

@ $14.95 per copy.

Quantity Discounts: 10–25   Copies   10%
                        26–50   Copies   15%
                        51–100 Copies   20%
                        101 +   Copies   25%

Total Cost: _____

Name: _____

Address: _____

City: _____ State: _____ Zip: _____

Telephone: _____ Fax: _____

E-mail: _____

Payment: Check_____ Money Order _____ Credit Card _____

Discover _____ AMEX _____ Master Card_____ Visa _____

Card Number: _____ Exp. Date: _____

0-595-33282-X

Breinigsville, PA USA
18 November 2009
227826BV00006B/50/A

9 780595 332823